*The
Evolution
of
Church Building*

Norwich Cathedral, Norfolk
The west front

Jack Bowyer

The Evolution of Church Building

Whitney Library of Design
an imprint of Watson-Guptill Publications
New York

First published in Great Britain 1977 by Crosby Lockwood Staples

First published in the United States of America in 1977
by the Whitney Library of Design,
an imprint of Watson-Guptill Publications
a division of Billboard Publications, Inc.
1515 Broadway, New York, New York 10036

Library of Congress Catalog Card No. 77–89256
ISBN 0–8230–7163–4

Printed in Great Britain

Contents

Preface

One of the most significant features of the English scene is the survival of so many places of Christian worship. A short journey through any county bears this out and at the same time indicates, within certain general regional characteristics, a breadth of variation on the original theme which typifies the English character – highly individual and disdainful of any form of standardisation.

One feature readily apparent to all but the most casual visitor is the genial relationship between local geology and the structure of many of our churches: in the chalklands of East Anglia and South East England flint, locally occurring both within the chalk and scattered over the surface of the fields, provides the material used with such mastery by local church builders; in Cornwall, the abundance of local granite has produced a strong, coarsely-moulded local idiom which is a dominant feature of this countryside.

However, the importance of ritual embodied in the Catholic Mass led to the development of a plan form which, in essence, varies little from cathedral to humble parish church. It is true that not all parishes were endowed with sufficient wealth or patronage fully to develop the plan form which is embodied in most of the greater churches; but many did so, altering, extending, demolishing and rebuilding over the centuries. New styles of decoration were superimposed on the earlier structure until today it is often difficult to date precisely many of the alterations.

The virtual cessation of church building in the early sixteenth century created a hiatus in the expression of rural craftsmanship, which was not to find again a comparable outlet. The explosion of house building in Tudor and Stuart times was carried out at a tempo vastly different from the leisurely pace of the mediaeval builders. Materials changed: brick took the place of stone in structural work, and the dearth of good oak led to the importation of Baltic softwoods. The visual excitement of the late Perpendicular fantasies was overtaken by the staid and correct classicism of Wren and his contemporaries. The craftsmanship was there, but the freedom of expression enjoyed by the mediaeval mason was now restricted and contained within a narrow classicism concerned more with conformity than with inspiration.

This period saw two waves of popular vandalism which, in their senseless and ignorant depravity, are almost unparalleled. The first was the almost total destruction of the monastic foundations and the breaking up of their vast collections of mediaeval art. Nearly one thousand of these churches were despoiled, most of them of superb quality. Those that remain can give us only a glimpse of the beauty that was wantonly destroyed. The second was a result of the narrow-minded ignorance of Puritanism when, at the time of the Civil War and after, stained glass windows and statuary were smashed in the pursuit of a more narrow religious approach to the worship of the same God.

Apathy and neglect were the features of the hundred years before the Gothic revival of the nineteenth century. Churches with absentee vicars fell into disrepair. With the new wave of building, their renovators, in the process of restoration, often destroyed features of interest and beauty in the cause of stylistic purity and uniformity. Their efforts are plain to see in many of our parish churches today. It was during this period that many new churches were built and also, with the increasing wealth and freedom enjoyed by Nonconformists, a great many chapels, especially in areas of growing population. This freedom extended to Catholics who, deprived of their churches at the Reformation, had worshipped in private until the construction of their new churches and cathedrals was permitted towards the close of the nineteenth century.

Today, thanks to legislation which requires parishes to repair and maintain their churches properly, the majority of our church buildings are safe for posterity. Careful and generally enlightened maintenance prohibits the return of the excesses of the Victorian restorers. Unfortunately, the same cannot be said of many of the more interesting early Nonconformist places of worship. Some of these, dating back to the seventeenth century and of considerable architectural taste and merit, have been allowed to fall into total disrepair.

For convenience, this book is divided into sections dealing with the growth of the monastic houses, the greater churches served by canons choral and not associated with any closed order, and the parish churches served since their foundation by clergy appointed by the Crown, the diocese or private patron. The growth of these churches and their ancillary buildings has been followed in some detail. A separate section describes methods of construction, the materials used and the way in which they were decorated. The structure is only half the building, however, and a complementary chapter describes the multitude of fittings and furniture considered necessary for the proper functioning of the whole for religious services. Any book dealing with the growth of the English church would be incomplete without a chapter describing the evolution of the Nonconformist community and their places of worship, many of which are buildings of great interest and beauty. It is hoped that this will be of interest to more conventional church visitors.

Many individual buildings are mentioned in the text, and these have been collated in an appendix that provides an index based, as far as possible, on county representation. It is hoped that this book will interest all those who visit and enjoy the beauties of the buildings that make up our heritage. If it encourages those who previously have missed one of the most satisfying of pastimes to discover a new dimension of English culture, an even greater degree of success may be claimed. For those whose travelling days are over, perhaps it will bring back happy memories of visits past.

Chapter One

*The
Greater
Churches*

Tewkesbury Abbey, Gloucestershire

The planning of a mediaeval great church, with provision for a multitude of complex services, accommodation for both worshippers and pilgrims together with the domestic buildings of the monastery, was a problem of great complexity. That it was usually solved without loss of beauty or dignity is due to the ingenuity and skill of the master builders.

A cathedral or minster church is the culmination of five centuries of organic growth, the final stage of a development which began in the catacombs of early Christian Rome and passed through the basilican plan form where the clergy sat around the eastern apse facing the congregation, with the bishop in his cathedra in the middle. By the eleventh century the monastic church of Western Europe had evolved into a large cruciform building, with well-developed transepts, surmounted by a low central tower.

The eleventh-century great church was divided into a number of separate and usually well-defined areas, each provided and used for specific purposes.

(i) The presbytery or sanctuary, containing the high altar, required at least two bays: one for the altar itself, freestanding on all sides, and one for the celebrant and staff of the Mass. The freestanding high altar is one distinguishing feature between the greater church and the parish church, although a few of the latter were considered of sufficient importance for this special provision (Newark, Nottinghamshire). Many twelfth-century presbyteries were planned with four bays, to accommodate the small matins altar often provided in front of the high altar. It was in the presbytery that the need for more room was early required and this generally comprised the first major extension.

(ii) The choir, placed west of the presbytery and usually two steps below its floor level, contained the stalls appropriated to the use of the monks or canons. Its length and position varied. With a short eastern limb of the church, the stalls were sometimes sited under the central crossing (Norwich, Norfolk; Peterborough, Cambridgeshire; Christchurch, Hampshire) but more often were immediately to the east of it. Most of the greater churches have been so extended that the stalls are arranged behind a screen placed across the east side of the crossing (Southwell, Nottinghamshire; Ely, Cambridgeshire; Exeter, Devon), and this is the form generally recognised as the typical English plan.

(iii) The retro-choir appeared in the twelfth and thirteenth centuries, when it assumed considerable size and importance as the repository of the shrine of the patron saint. It involved the replanning of the eastern end of the church to allow the shrine to be visible in its splendour beyond the high altar. The earliest known example is at Canterbury, and was extended after the fire of 1174 to form the Chapel of St Thomas Becket. Other cathedrals followed suit (Winchester, Hampshire; Worcester).

(iv) The nave, or western portion, of the church was often of great length, especially in post-Conquest Benedictine foundations (St Albans, Hertfordshire; Winchester, Hampshire). Later churches were built with smaller naves – it seems likely that the vast pillared halls were found to be, in practice, far larger than was ever required, and perhaps the question of maintenance also became a major consideration.

(v) Transepts remained a separate and distinctive part of the greater church plan, even though in parish churches they were often replaced by aisle and chapel extensions. While the symbolism of the cruciform church may have been of influence, the main reason for the retention of transepts was their buttressing value for the central tower, an important feature of the English great church. Main transepts were often originally built without aisles but with eastern apsidal chapels (St Albans, Hertfordshire). Later examples usually had aisles on the east side only, serving as chapels separated by solid walls (Ely, Cambridgeshire) and later by screens.

Western aisles, originally designed as chapels, for which they were generally found to be unsuitable due to

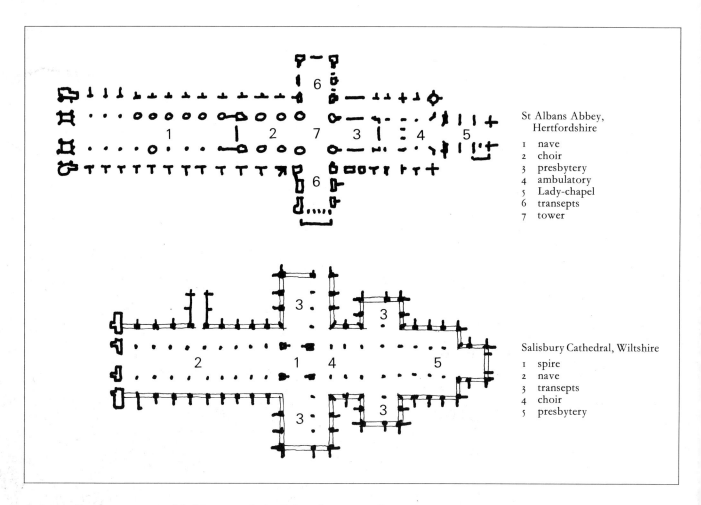

St Albans Abbey,
Hertfordshire

1 nave
2 choir
3 presbytery
4 ambulatory
5 Lady-chapel
6 transepts
7 tower

Salisbury Cathedral, Wiltshire

1 spire
2 nave
3 transepts
4 choir
5 presbytery

their small size, were provided in a number of churches (Beverley and York, Yorkshire; Wells, Somerset). At Winchester the transepts are provided with aisles on sides and end, probably serving to connect upper chapels or continue the triforium passage.

Western transepts were provided in some instances but were soon superseded by eastern transepts, which became a feature of English design by the thirteenth century. Probably the first eastern transepts were those of the Cluniac Priory of Lewes in Sussex (c. 1100), but the earliest surviving example is at Canterbury; here the eastern transepts project farther than the main transepts and each is provided with a pair of apsidal chapels, as against single chapels only in the western. Other, later examples are to be found: pairs with twin chapels separated originally by screens (Hereford Cathedral), with eastern aisles (Salisbury, Hampshire) and square on plan (Worcester). This feature may be regarded as an important part of the favourite English eastern termination and, when set in line with the high altar, gives both

Worcester Cathedral

dignity and an impressive appearance, especially as most eastern transepts are of full height (Worcester; Salisbury, Wiltshire). Where they are lower than the height of the choir, the loss of effect is at once apparent (Wells, Somerset).

(vi) The chapter-house and cloister form one of the characteristic features of the English great church – particularly the polygonal chapter-house, ranging from the Romanesque at Worcester, with a central pillar, to that of Wells, constructed over a vaulted lower storey. Some chapter-houses are constructed without a central pier (Southwell, Nottinghamshire; York Minster). The ma-

jority are octagonal, but that at Hereford was decagonal and the vanished example at Abbey Dore, Herefordshire, had twelve sides. The cloister was the chief day-accommodation of the monks and most of those surviving date from the thirteenth to fifteenth centuries. The earliest is the Romanesque example at Canterbury and other fine cloisters can be found at Gloucester, Westminster Abbey and Norwich.

The transformation of the Romanesque Benedictine church into the English cathedral took centuries of change and alteration. The plan of the Benedictine abbey

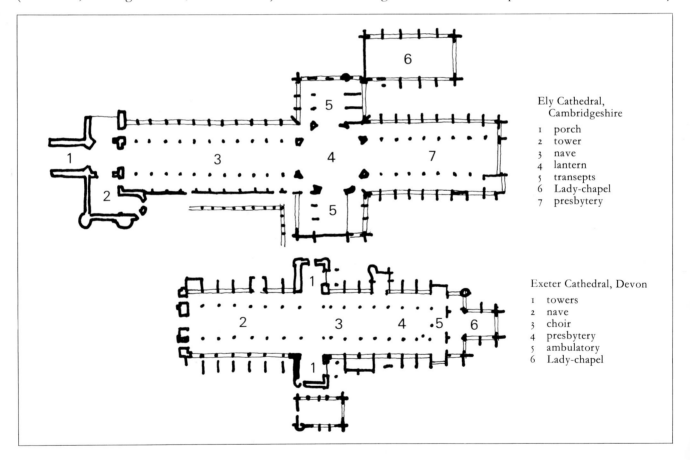

Ely Cathedral,
  Cambridgeshire
1 porch
2 tower
3 nave
4 lantern
5 transepts
6 Lady-chapel
7 presbytery

Exeter Cathedral, Devon
1 towers
2 nave
3 choir
4 presbytery
5 ambulatory
6 Lady-chapel

generally followed those of contemporary abbeys in Normandy, such as St Nicholas, Caen. These were built over a period of at least 100 years, the vast naves added to, bay after bay, without much regard to new developments in design. Many of the great Romanesque naves (Ely; Norwich; Peterborough) were being completed at the same time as the commencement of work on the new nave at Wells in Somerset or the choir of St Hugh at Lincoln. Original Benedictine plans survive (Tewkesbury and Gloucester, Gloucestershire), where the Norman apses were remodelled in the fourteenth century without much alteration to the original plan.

The English Romanesque greater church, characterised by its length, was usually surmounted by a central tower over the transeptal crossing (St Albans, Hertfordshire). Occasionally twin western towers were provided (Durham; Southwell, Nottinghamshire; Chichester, Sussex). Alone of English cathedrals, Exeter was provided with flanking towers raised above the original transepts.

The eastern termination of three parallel apses is of great antiquity, dating back to early Christian days, and survives in many churches in Italy. The Norman cathedral of Hereford terminated in such a manner but this was found to afford little space for ritual ceremonies

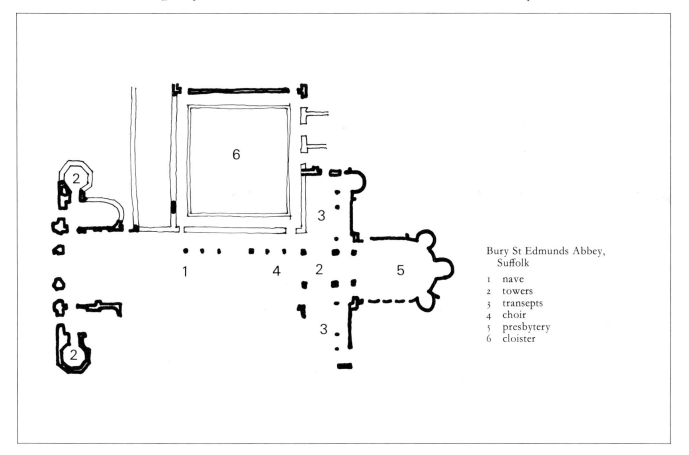

Bury St Edmunds Abbey,
    Suffolk

1   nave
2   towers
3   transepts
4   choir
5   presbytery
6   cloister

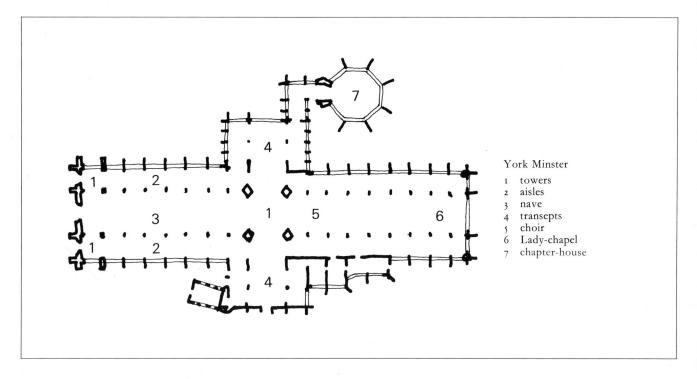

York Minster

1 towers
2 aisles
3 nave
4 transepts
5 choir
6 Lady-chapel
7 chapter-house

and none for the processions which were such a feature of mediaeval religion. An improvement was the construction of a passageway, outside the central apse, from which radiated chapels; this design, originating from the Byzantine churches of south-east Europe and finding much favour in France, was introduced into England at Bury St Edmunds, Suffolk, and the Cluniac Priory at Lewes, Sussex.

Within a few years, however, the construction of Cistercian and Augustinian abbeys brought a new design concept to the eastern end of Romanesque churches. The apses were swept away and the square, eastern termination, a typically English feature, evolved in its many varieties.

The need to provide for processions, the development of multiple altars and the veneration of the hosts of pilgrims at the shrine containing the mortal remains of the saint that each great building had acquired, all demanded considerable eastern extension to most major churches in England. It was here that chapels were provided for the use of the numerous canons and monastic brethren to whom the high altar, used mainly for the more important occasions of the Mass, was not available. Whereas the French provided their chapels in a radiating semicircle neatly tucked between the great projecting buttresses that absorbed the thrust from the roof, the English cathedral incorporated chapels and altars distributed throughout the eastern termination and transepts (Salisbury Cathedral, Hampshire). Chantry and family chapels were usually constructed between choir and nave arcade piers (Winchester Cathedral, Hampshire) as generally, except for King's College Chapel, Cambridge, the projection of the buttresses was not sufficient to accommodate them.

The first cathedral to extend eastwards was Canterbury, only a few years after the completion of the original church. The choir of eleven bays which resulted, and which was at the time the longest in Europe, was destroyed by fire in 1174; the rounded chevet is the final result of work conceived in 1180 as the addition of the great chapel (now known as the Trinity Chapel) built to receive the shrine of St Thomas Becket. This exceptional feature was not followed by the English cathedral builders, who preferred the provision of a large chapel behind the high altar.

The typically English eastern termination is to be found at Hereford Cathedral. Here the three eastern apses were swept away in favour of a feretory chapel having a processional path giving access to pairs of square-ended eastern chapels with, beyond, a large projecting eastern chapel. Chichester Cathedral was provided with a new retro-choir in the twelfth century and a Lady-chapel in the thirteenth. The idea reached its peak in the construction, from 1228, of Salisbury Cathedral, the only great church built entirely and completely in one homogeneous style, and at Wells in Somerset. These cathedrals reflect the ideas and designs of the south and west of England, but northern builders had a simpler method of reaching the same ideal. Here the Lady-chapel terminating the eastern end of the church was constructed to the full height of the choir (York Minster), providing a spacious dignity and splendour which is lacking in the southern examples.

The cathedral became a screen-divided hall, arcaded from west to east and, except for the projecting transepts, differing little from the great parish churches which were being constructed or reconstructed in the fourteenth century (Halifax, Yorkshire; St Nicholas, Kings Lynn, Norfolk). A variation found only in the Northern Province provides for the addition of a large hall placed across the whole east end of the church, providing ample space for a number of altars (Fountains Abbey, Yorkshire; Durham Cathedral).

Canterbury Cathedral crypt

Canterbury Cathedral crypt

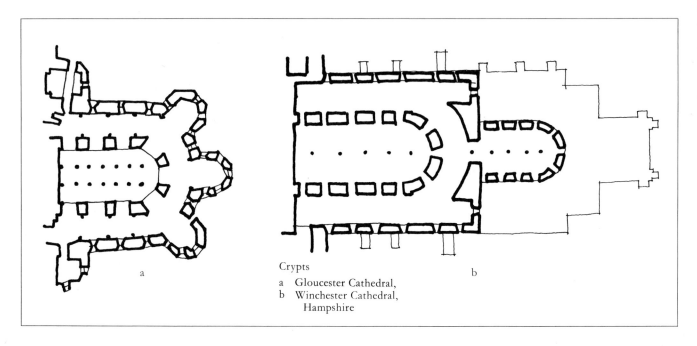

Crypts
a   Gloucester Cathedral,
b   Winchester Cathedral,
    Hampshire

The Cistercians, with their individualistic outlook on church building, began to evolve a more spacious eastern termination. This comprised an aisled eastern extension of four to six bays with an eastern range of chapels usually divided by low walls (Byland Abbey and Jervaulx Abbey, Yorkshire). Probably the most interesting survivor is at Abbey Dore, Herefordshire, dating from c. 1190. By now the apsidal east end was almost extinct, although several examples antedate this period. Westminster Abbey, designed in the French manner, found no imitators. The apsed choir at Pershore, Worcestershire, built c. 1223, survives in the sadly truncated church, and at Beaulieu Abbey, Hampshire (c. 1246) the most complete chevet in England was constructed with a fringe of ten radiating chapels, divided by stone screen walls, inside the main wall of the apse. Never popular, apart from these examples and some which have been reconstructed with English eastern terminations (Lincoln Cathedral), the Continental chevet was discarded by cathedral builders.

The crypt was a Romanesque feature which failed to establish itself as an integral part of greater English churches and died out in the general rebuilding by the end of the twelfth century. The only examples after this date were constructed at Rochester in Kent (which was probably erected upon earlier footings), in Glasgow and in the Metropolitan cathedral of Old St Paul's. Several early crypts have survived, mainly in smaller churches (Hexham, Northumberland; Wing, Buckinghamshire; Repton, Derbyshire). Romanesque crypts in larger churches are more common (Ripon, Yorkshire); at Canterbury, three spacious Norman crypts survive, one as a Lady-chapel originally the repository of great treasures.

Crypts often provide important evidence of the original termination of the founding church, lying, as they usually do, under the original high altar. Gloucester Cathedral, we find, originally had three radiating chapels,

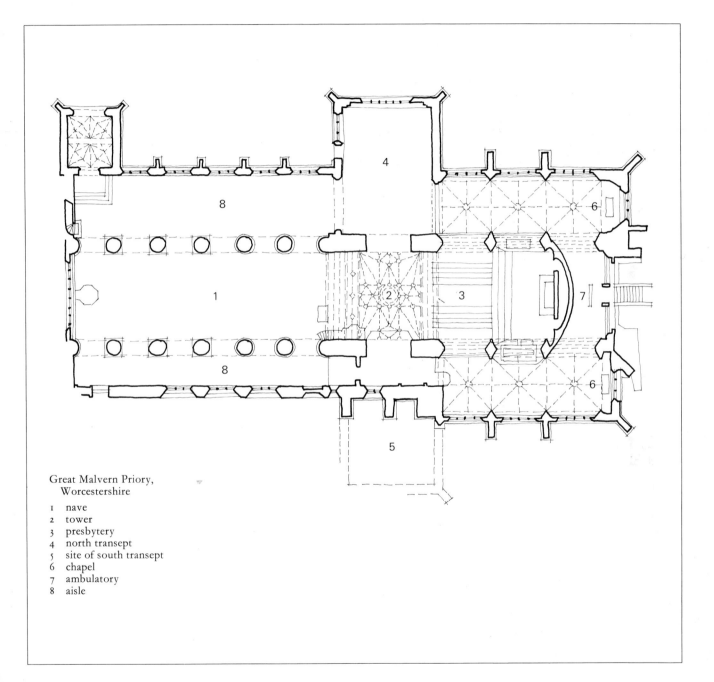

Great Malvern Priory,
    Worcestershire

1 nave
2 tower
3 presbytery
4 north transept
5 site of south transept
6 chapel
7 ambulatory
8 aisle

St John the Baptist, Cirencester, Gloucestershire
The south porch

St Mary the Virgin, Oxford
The south porch

Winchester an ambulatory with two small square-sided chapels and a projecting apsidal Lady-chapel. Crypts were, however, inconvenient for processions and liable to be damp and difficult to light and ventilate, and they gradually disappeared from new church plans.

Many churches of size and architectural importance did not aspire to the prominence of the major cathedrals and abbeys. Some incorporated a Lady-chapel, but without the processional path (Great Malvern, Worcestershire; Binham Priory, Norfolk). In others, the choir was aisled but not the presbytery, processions having to pass before the high altar (Walsingham, Norfolk; Wimborne Minster, Dorset). A further development provided for an unaisled eastern limb, the choir proper being provided in the crossing and the eastern nave. This typical Cistercian arrangement is also found in Premonstratensian churches (Bayham Abbey, Lamberhurst, Kent) and also in many remote churches throughout the country (Brecon Cathedral, Powys; Llanthony Priory, Gwent; Lindisfarne Priory, Northumberland).

By the middle of the fourteenth century, greater church planning and conventional church building had come to an end due to the destruction of human life by the Black Death. The important forces in church building became the wealthy merchant and the craft guild, enlarging and rebuilding the parish churches of their native towns – the great churches of East Anglia and the wide-aisled screen churches of Devon.

Fifteenth-century churches were given smaller choirs and larger naves (Bath Abbey, Avon) and rebuildings of this century produced eastern ends having enclosed choirs, with enough room for processions only at the aisle ends (Christchurch Priory, Hampshire). The work on the greater churches at this period was that of remodelling rather than of reconstruction, usually within the original dimensions, mostly impressive and incorporating the highest standards of skilful design and craftsmanship.

With the Reformation, the building of great churches ceased. Minor extensions and alterations were occasionally carried out, such as the Baroque south porch with barley-sugar columns added in 1637 by Nicholas Stone to St Mary the Virgin, Oxford, and the Corinthian portico to Old St Paul's by Inigo Jones. A new impetus to church building was given by the disastrous fire which gutted the City of London in 1666 destroying, along with over fifty mediaeval city churches, the great Metropolitan cathedral of St Paul.

Before the fire, Christopher Wren had prepared a report in favour of drastic reconstruction of the old building, then in a serious structural condition: the interior was to be refaced using classical motifs and the nave vault replaced with saucer domes. All these ideas were cast aside with the burning of the building. In 1669 Wren was appointed Surveyor to the Office of Works and began the detailed work involved in the preparation of designs for a new cathedral. By 1673 a model of the design was ready, showing a building designed in the form of a Greek cross with an extension to the west to form an entrance portico. Over the central area a dome was to be constructed, carried on eight great piers. The plan was not favoured by the ecclesiastical authorities, who favoured a more conventional design from which developed the Warrant plan of a Latin cross – substantially the building that was eventually constructed. The foundation stone was laid on 21 June 1675 and by the end of 1711 the new cathedral was completed, the whole structure having been erected within Wren's lifetime. Today, the building has been cleaned and refurbished and stands much as it did at the beginning of the eighteenth century.

During the nineteenth century much restoration work and rebuilding was carried out on the great churches. Many, such as Westminster Abbey and Worcester Cathedral, were entirely refaced. Some which had partially collapsed were rebuilt, often with new additions, and their original architectural styles sadly altered (Hereford Cathedral). Many larger parish churches

became cathedrals in newly created dioceses (St Michael's, Coventry, Warwickshire; All Saints, Wakefield, Yorkshire). New buildings rose where the need occasioned, notably Truro Cathedral (1879–87) designed by J. L. Pearson.

The renewal of Catholic religious freedom in the nineteenth century brought a number of new cathedrals to serve the Roman Catholic faith. Augustus Pugin designed the cathedral of St George, Southwark, London (1840–48), which was subsequently rebuilt after severe damage suffered during the Second World War. The Metropolitan Cathedral of Westminster was built in the Byzantine style by J. F. Bentley (1895–1910); the view of the main front has recently been greatly improved by new developments and roadworks. In 1960 work commenced, after two false starts since Pugin began work in 1853, on the new Cathedral of Christ the King, Liverpool, to the designs of Frederick Gibberd.

The Anglicans were engaged in similar work. In 1901 Giles Gilbert Scott began work on the new Liverpool Cathedral, constructed in stone, which, if completed, will be second in size only to St Peter's, Rome. The new diocese of Guildford has been provided by Edward Maufe with a brick cathedral begun in 1936; St Michael's, Coventry, destroyed by bombing in 1940, has been rebuilt in stone-faced reinforced concrete by Basil Spence.

St Paul's Cathedral, London

Chapter Two

Abbeys
and
Conventual
Houses

The basic order of western monasticism was the Benedictine, on which all the others were founded. There were, however, in mediaeval England a number of other orders whose interpretation of the rule as laid down by St Benedict affected the planning and architectural treatment of their abbeys. The original conception of Benedictine rule was one of austerity, but by the tenth century this was challenged at Cluny, where the monks began to develop an elaborate ritual which was to require a fine setting for its performance. The Cluniac order quickly grew popular and prospered. One of its lay admirers was William the Conquerer, during whose reign the Cluniac Priory of Lewes, Sussex, was founded by William de Warenne. Almost completely destroyed in 1539, as was the Cluniac Priory of Thetford, the fine west front of Castle Acre Priory, also in Norfolk, remains to illustrate the quality of architectural work incorporated in buildings of this order.

Monks were not in holy orders but were laymen who, having taken the habit, lived in a community under its rule. The priests who staffed the cathedral churches were called canons and lived in a community represented by the cathedral close (Hereford; Wells, Somerset); these canons secular were not under the discipline of a rule. The foundation of the Augustinian order provided for canons regular who, although they lived in priories, were not strictly enclosed but were free to go about their work in parishes in common with the parish priests.

The Augustinians were generally educated men, in contrast to the members of most other orders, and this advantage is to be seen in their houses, which incorporated many new ideas and improvements. Their churches, of fine quality, concentrated on choir and presbytery with less emphasis on the nave, which was usually only nominal. Many of these churches have survived (Waltham Abbey, Essex; Christchurch Priory, Hampshire; Cirencester, Gloucestershire; Thornton Abbey, Lincolnshire) and after 1539 three became cathedrals of the New Foundation (Bristol, Avon; Oxford; Carlisle, Cumbria).

Within the Benedictine order reforming movements arose which advocated strict observance of the original rule of austerity and poverty. These views coalesced in the Abbey of Citeaux in Burgundy and resulted in the foundation of the Cistercian order, which was to become of great importance and power in England. The Cistercians set aside all wealth and founded their abbeys in remote areas, where the land was worked solely under their direction. As they found it impossible to carry out all the work themselves they admitted lay brothers, who enjoyed the privilege of a sheltered life in the well-ordered community.

Gloucester Cathedral

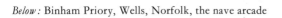

Below: Binham Priory, Wells, Norfolk, the nave arcade   *Right:* Castle Acre Priory, Swaffham, Norfolk, the west front

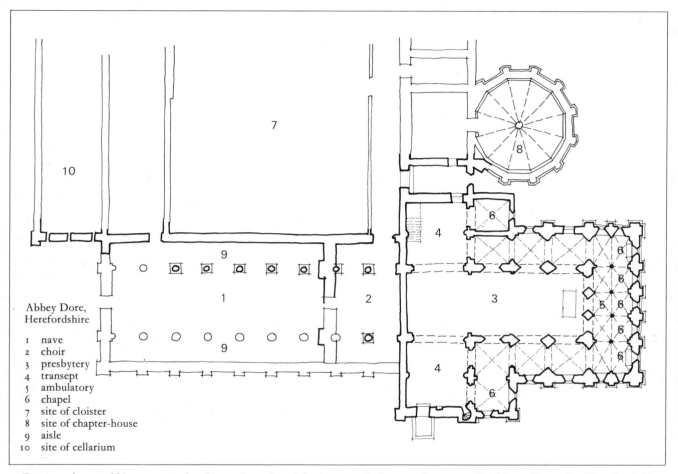

Abbey Dore,
Herefordshire

1 nave
2 choir
3 presbytery
4 transept
5 ambulatory
6 chapel
7 site of cloister
8 site of chapter-house
9 aisle
10 site of cellarium

During the twelfth century the Cistercians flourished and, changing their views on worldly wealth, began to improve their buildings to make them the objects of admiration which they are today. Of the foundation house of Waverley Abbey in Surrey only a few grey stones now remain, but many Cistercian abbeys have survived in part or almost complete (Buildwas Abbey, Shropshire; Fountains Abbey and Rievaulx Abbey, Yorkshire; Tintern Abbey, Gwent). Two Cistercian houses have remained in use as parish churches: the nave of Margam Abbey in Glamorganshire and the presbytery of Abbey Dore in Herefordshire.

The aesthetic appeal of the Cistercian order encouraged the canons regular to institute the order of white canons or Premonstratensians. This order built many fine abbeys in the country, copying the Augustinian plan of a nave incorporating a single aisle. Several of these churches remain in part, notably Bayham Abbey in Sussex and Halesowen Abbey in Worcestershire. In this order lay brothers who helped on the farms were accommodated outside the claustral buildings, as no lay-brother houses were provided.

Buildwas Abbey, near Ironbridge, Shropshire

Bath Abbey, Avon

Most orders founded houses for women who lived under the same rule as the men and whose houses followed similar plans. Some of these had magnificent churches (Romsey Abbey, Hampshire; Minster-in-Sheppey, Kent), now in use as parish churches. The Gilbertine order, peculiarly English, provided double houses containing nuns together with canons who officiated at Mass: the church was central, with cloisters and conventual buildings on either side. Sempringham in Lincolnshire and Walton, Yorkshire, are the best-known of these priories.

THE CHURCH

The early Benedictine order did not envisage the construction of a church, merely an oratory which was reserved for prayerful worship. The church plans of the period were developing from the Byzantine ideal of a central dome carried on piers with short nave, sanctuary and transepts all enclosed within a square, to the long-axial basilican plan which became the standard arrangement for the western church. The division between the monastic and lay portions of the church was rigidly

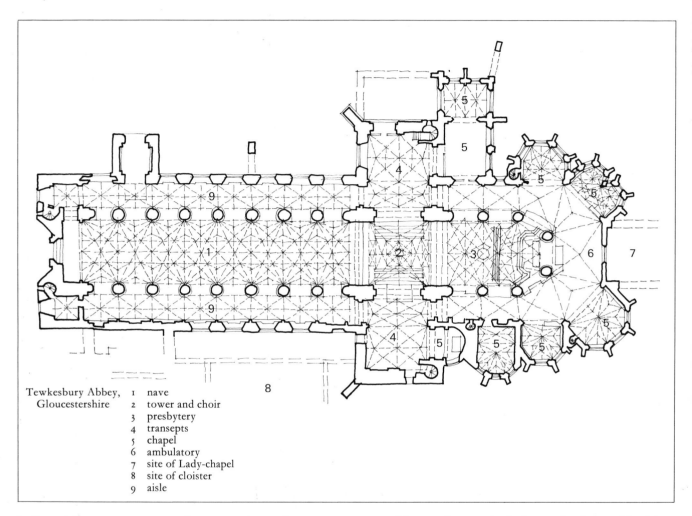

Tewkesbury Abbey,
Gloucestershire

1 nave
2 tower and choir
3 presbytery
4 transepts
5 chapel
6 ambulatory
7 site of Lady-chapel
8 site of cloister
9 aisle

indicated by a stone screen, the monastic rood screen. A number of these have survived the Reformation (Malmesbury Abbey, Wiltshire; Crowland Abbey, Lincolnshire). East of the rood screen was a screen known as the pulpitum which marked the western limit of the monks' choir, the space between being known as the retro-choir and used, it is said, to accommodate sick monks unable to stand through the long choir services.

The choir itself was designed as an enclosed compart-ment with seats for monks facing each other and backing onto the pulpitum and, at the east end, the high altar. Between the seats and the high altar was an open space known as the presbytery, usually sited beneath the high arched crossing supporting the lantern and tower of the church. At the extreme end of the choir was the reredos, usually sculptured and canopied in stone (Winchester Cathedral, Hampshire; St Albans, Hertfordshire), but today devoid of the statuary once contained. Beside the altar was a group of stone seats with elaborate canopies and carved details. These 'sedilia', which also appeared in parish churches, were the permanent seats provided for the priests officiating at Mass (Selby Abbey, Yorkshire; Tewkesbury, Gloucestershire).

The usual eastern termination of the abbey was a square gable-end with three apses (Hereford Cathedral). The Continental termination known as the chevet, mentioned in Chapter 1, was introduced c. 1100: a ring of apses projected from a semi-circular aisle, providing a processional route behind the high altar (Tewkesbury Abbey, Gloucestershire; Norwich Cathedral, Norfolk; Westminster Abbey). However, this plan incorporating an apsidal end never gained popularity; from the first the Cistercians would have nothing to do with it, preferring the Celtic gable-end termination, but with the east wall supported on arches with an aisle returned across the east end. At Byland Abbey in Yorkshire this aisle wall was filled in with five chapels; at Abbey Dore the aisle was extended a further bay to the east, with the roof carried on a row of slender columns to provide a series of five chapels accommodated under a separate roof. This development reached its climax in the Chapel of the Nine Altars at Fountains Abbey in Yorkshire.

DOMESTIC BUILDINGS

The Dorter

The domestic quarters of the monks were usually set at right angles to the abbey church, either attached to or following the alignment of the transept on the south side. The dormitory or dorter on the main floor was reached by a stone stair inside the transept wall leading to a doorway high up in the church wall (Hexham Priory, Northumberland). This was known as the 'night stair', the 'day stair' usually being at the other end of the dorter (Tintern Abbey, Gwent). Sometimes the intrusion of the chapter-house between the church and the dorter made the provision of a night stair difficult, and one stair had to suffice.

The number of individuals accommodated varied from a minimum of twelve to probably 100. At Fountains Abbey, Yorkshire, the total number of monks and lay brothers may well have exceeded 500, but after the Black Death of 1348 the lay brothers disappeared never to return. Large numbers of individuals presented problems of sanitation. The rere-dorter, or lavatory, was attached to the monks' quarters and consisted of a two-storey structure with a passage through which ran a stream of water in a stone-lined channel. On the first floor a row of seats, separated by screens, was set over the open drain. The rere-dorter was constructed at either the end or centre of the dorter on the east side, farthest from the cloister. The number of seats varied with the size of the foundation, Castle Acre in Norfolk being provided with twelve, Canterbury Cathedral originally having fifty-five (probably serving up to 1000 individuals). Sometimes the abbot's house was sited at the east end of the rere-dorter so that his guests could use the accommodation. The infirmary hall, often placed to the north, formed the side of a court with covered access to the rere-dorter for active patients. Separate provision was made for the lay brothers.

Several examples of the monks' dorter survive, probably the best being at Cleeve Abbey in Somerset and Battle Abbey in Sussex.

The Frater

The monks' house was a large two-storeyed structure raised on a simple vaulted undercroft and usually approached by an open stair. Its windows were small and unglazed, in complete contrast to the great hall or refectory (frater) where all monks gathered at mealtimes to be served from the central kitchen. The monastic frater incorporated a dais and high table for the abbot, below which the brothers sat at long refectory tables

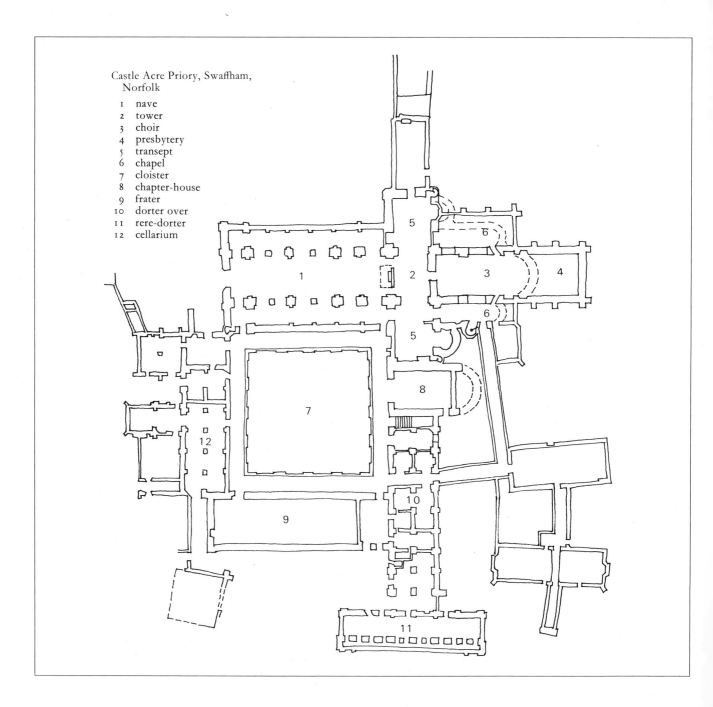

Castle Acre Priory, Swaffham,
Norfolk

1 nave
2 tower
3 choir
4 presbytery
5 transept
6 chapel
7 cloister
8 chapter-house
9 frater
10 dorter over
11 rere-dorter
12 cellarium

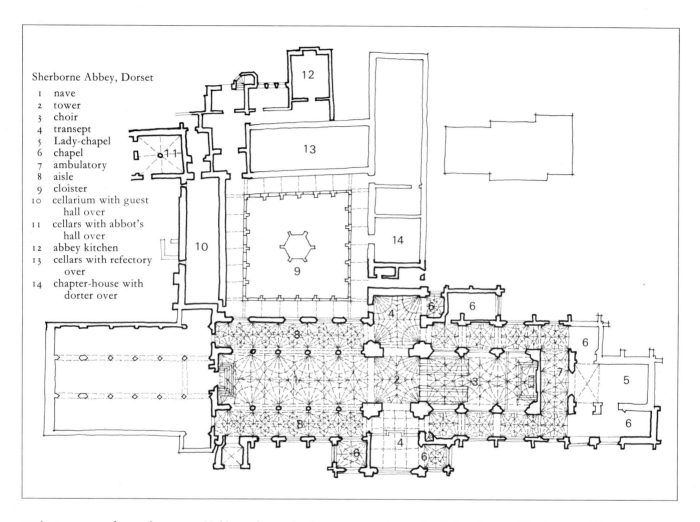

Sherborne Abbey, Dorset

1 nave
2 tower
3 choir
4 transept
5 Lady-chapel
6 chapel
7 ambulatory
8 aisle
9 cloister
10 cellarium with guest
    hall over
11 cellars with abbot's
    hall over
12 abbey kitchen
13 cellars with refectory
    over
14 chapter-house with
    dorter over

set in two rows down the room. Halfway down the frater was a stone pulpit set in the wall, approached by a stair and usually finely decorated, which was used for mealtime readings. Examples have survived at Fountains Abbey, Yorkshire, at Chester Cathedral and at Beaulieu Abbey in Hampshire, where the frater has been converted into the parish church.

The monks' hall was usually sited on the south side of the church, separated from it by a court and connected to the end of the dorter (Sherborne Abbey, Dorset). The kitchen was usually at the west end of the frater and connected to it by a serving hatch (Tintern Abbey, Gwent), and beside the door was a laver or washing place. This was served by a lead pipe from the conduit which, having first supplied the kitchen, passed eastward to flush the rere-dorter. The laver usually comprised a stone trough set in a niche under a wide arch, often with towel cupboards nearby (Gloucester Cathedral).

The Cellarer Range

The original intention of monastic rule was to isolate the inmate from worldly temptations. With the church, monks' house and frater forming three sides of a square, it was logical to complete the enclosure. This was effected by the construction of a range of rooms used for the storage of foodstuffs, cloth, fuel, etc. The store controller was known as the 'cellarer' and the buildings became known as the 'cellarer range'.

To provide access to this whole enclosed area, or cloister, a vaulted passage was contrived close to the junction of the cellarer range and the church (Fountains Abbey, Yorkshire). Within this passage, the 'outer parlour', took place any contact required with the outside world.

Above the cellarer's range was accommodation for the abbot and his guests; after the twelfth century, separate lodging was usually provided for the abbot but guests were often still accommodated over the cellarium (Sherborne Abbey, Dorset). Often the abbot's house developed as a wing constructed at right angles to the south end of the cellarium, providing added architectural interest to the west front of the abbey.

The Kitchen

The requirement that all members of the order should dine together entailed the provision of a kitchen. Unfortunately, few kitchens have survived in any detail, the only one of any importance being the remarkable structure at Glastonbury, Somerset. This square building, now standing alone and apart, incorporates under its vaulted roof four great hearths set in the angles, with flues rising within the masonary to meet in an elaborate central turret. The kitchen was designed to cook whole carcases which, as meat was not part of the monastic diet, would have been used in the infirmary to supplement the diet of the sick and in the hospitium for the entertainment of the abbot's guests. The size of the kitchen at Glastonbury gives evidence of the importance and popularity of this abbey. The placing of the kitchen near to the abbot's house, the infirmary and the hospitium demonstrates a sense of economy as the same cooks could provide a central service to all three buildings. In smaller houses the kitchen was constructed at the lower end of the frater, reasonably close to the cellarium (Tintern Abbey, Gwent).

The Cloister

The cloister was the real home of the monk, used as a retreat, a study and a place to walk and meditate. Originally the sides of the central court formed by the principal abbey buildings were provided with external corridors, called pentices, passing along the east and west sides to give access to the various rooms and joining them to the doorways leading into the church. The addition of a pentice on the south side would provide a covered sunny walk. The original cloisters were merely pent roofs with the eaves carried on timber posts, as in an agricultural linhay. By the twelfth century this was being replaced by miniature arcades incorporating arches set in pairs to carry the masonry (Little Cloister, Canterbury, Kent). With the introduction of lead roofing, the pitch was flattened, the outer wall raised and the whole designed as a fine arcade.

In the fourteenth century the cloister was transformed by filling in the arches with tracery and glass and replacing the timber ceiling with elaborate vaulting supported externally by high pinnacled buttresses (Salisbury Cathedral, Wiltshire; Norwich Cathedral, Norfolk). At Gloucester the masons made each cloister bay into a study or carrel, lit through the tracery. Few remains of abbey cloisters survive except those at Lacock Abbey in Wiltshire where, although the church has completely vanished, the cloister and claustral buildings have survived as a private house.

Fountains Abbey, Ripon, Yorkshire
The cellarer undercroft

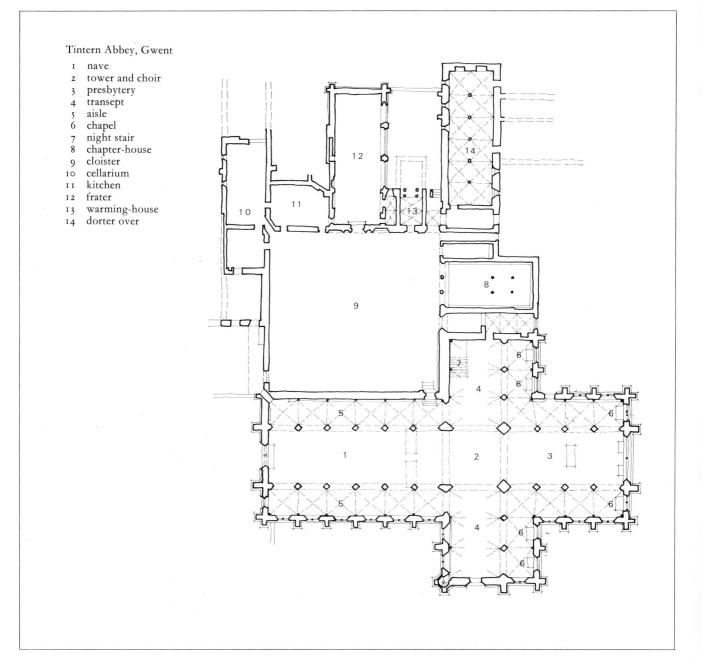

Tintern Abbey, Gwent

1 nave
2 tower and choir
3 presbytery
4 transept
5 aisle
6 chapel
7 night stair
8 chapter-house
9 cloister
10 cellarium
11 kitchen
12 frater
13 warming-house
14 dorter over

The Chapter-house

In monastic houses the abbot was elected by the order and governed in conclave with the community. Each house needed a hall in which matters of religion and administration could be discussed. By the time the monastic plan had reached this country, the chapter-house was the building second only in importance to the church, always sited next to it and generally accessible from the south or cloister transept. In the Cistercian houses the chapter-house usually formed part of the dorter range and was rectangular in plan, the roof supported by pillars (Tintern Abbey, Gwent; Forde Abbey, Somerset). This plan was also adopted by the Benedictines (Sherborne Abbey, Dorset).

By the fourteenth century separate chapter-houses became the rule – polygonal stone lanterns with their external walls filled with coloured glass, their vaulted roofs supported on a central column (Westminster Abbey). In older foundations the chapter-house was linked to the cloister by a vestibule formed from the original rectangular chapter-house.

The Infirmary

Once a monk entered the abbey he usually left it only through the inner parlour, or slype, to the cemetery. This passage (for this is what the slype was in practice) also gave access to the infirmary which provided, with its own kitchen and small refectory, accommodation for sick or old monks. The infirmary was often a large building and usually provided with a chapel at one end, for the use of its inmates, and a lodging for the infirmarer so that he could keep in close contact with his patients.

Many infirmary buildings were constructed around courtyards where convalescent patients could have their own promenade for exercise; 'pentices' were usually provided to give covered access to the separate rooms and thus this promenade could also be made under cover

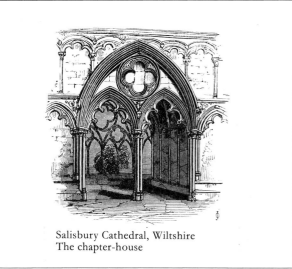

Salisbury Cathedral, Wiltshire
The chapter-house

(Fountains Abbey and Rievaulx Abbey, Yorkshire; Westminster Abbey). The little cloister at Much Wenlock Priory, Shropshire, is still complete and its east side comprises the fifteenth-century prior's lodging, with its fine stone panelled façade, incorporating a lodging for the infirmarer. The Augustinians usually varied this arrangement by providing the infirmary, or little cloister, on the south side of the frater; this arrangement was followed at Llanthony Priory in Gwent, where the infirmary hall is now used as the parish church, the infirmary chapel forming the chancel.

The Abbots' Lodging

The elevation of a monk to the position of abbot brought him to a position of great power, close to that of the peerage. He was responsible for the spiritual and temporal sides of monastic life, involved in the entertainment of persons of rank and quality and often in political issues. By the end of the twelfth century his position was such as to require the provision of lodging separate from that of the other brethren and during the following

The Priory, Much Wenlock, Shropshire
The chapter-house arcade

century a separate house was provided for the accommodation of the abbot. Meals were no problem, as the abbot took these at his high table in the frater, but the provision of a privy chamber where he could sleep and interview visitors was essential. Originally this was provided in the upper storey of the cellarer range, over the outer parlour, with a window looking into the church. Visitors were housed over the cellarer range, between the abbot's lodging and the frater.

The siting of a separate house for the abbot was governed by the position of the abbey kitchen and the provision of sanitary arrangements. Two situations presented themselves as suitable: the west end of the frater, at its junction with the cellarium (Sherborne Abbey, Dorset); or as part of the infirmary block around the little cloister, as at Mulcheney Abbey, Somerset, where the building incorporates a staircase leading up to the abbot's hall, complete with its elaborate carved fireplace. The prior's house at Much Wenlock, Shropshire, is similarly situated and is probably the best surviving example of mediaeval domestic architecture of the fifteenth century.

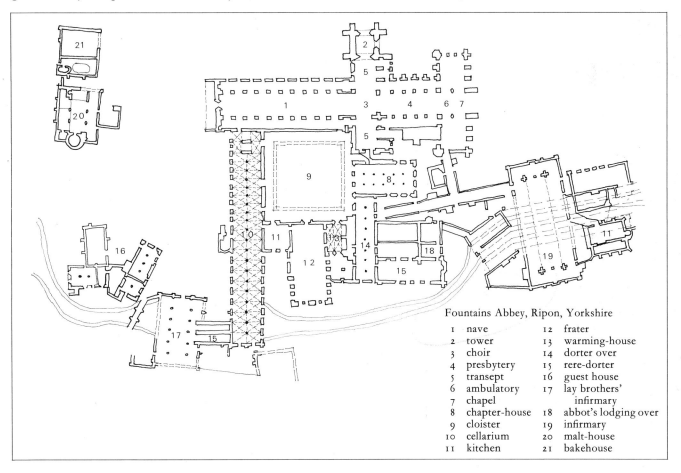

Fountains Abbey, Ripon, Yorkshire

1	nave	12	frater
2	tower	13	warming-house
3	choir	14	dorter over
4	presbytery	15	rere-dorter
5	transept	16	guest house
6	ambulatory	17	lay brothers'
7	chapel		infirmary
8	chapter-house	18	abbot's lodging over
9	cloister	19	infirmary
10	cellarium	20	malt-house
11	kitchen	21	bakehouse

The Great Court

The centre of the non-religious effort of the abbey was in its outer court. The outer parlour opened not directly into the open street but into a walled enclosure called the great court, accessible only to those of the public having business with the abbey. Access to the nave or public part of the church was by either the west door or a north porch (pre-supposing the cloister to be sited in its normal position on the south side of the church), and to any shrine at the east end of the church, through the north transept. The north and west sides of the church, therefore, were exposed to public access, the rest were within the abbey precincts.

Within the court were carried out the usual secular operations associated with the maintenance of a large community, and it accommodated the granary, bakehouse, brewery, masons' lodges and carpenters' and glaziers' shops. Here also was the smithy where all the ironwork associated with the abbey was fabricated. The court gave access to the guest-house forming part of the cellarium, the abbot's house and the almonry. On the north side of the abbey church there was some-times provided a parish church with a cemetery for the use of the parishioners; the best surviving example of this arrangement is St Margaret's, Westminster with Westminster Abbey.

The Gatehouse

Access to the court was provided by the great gatehouse, a feature of architectural importance of which many survive (Battle Abbey, Sussex; Michelham Priory, Sussex; Bury St Edmunds, Suffolk). Often a small wicket gate is incorporated to serve as an entrance for individuals on foot. Sometimes the gatehouses were used as prisons (St Albans, Hertfordshire) and that of the Benedictine Abbey of Ewenny in Glamorgan was fortified to provide greater protection in a region renowned for its lawlessness. The gatehouse of St Osyth's Priory in Essex was designed as a house and, after the Suppression of the Monasteries, continued to be used for this purpose. Its flint infilling and flushwork are outstanding in an area where this work is common.

Glastonbury Abbey, Somerset
The abbot's kitchen

Chapter Three

Parish
Churches

EVOLUTION OF PLAN

Virtually all English parish churches founded before the twelfth century can be traced back to one of three basic plan types:

Two-cell plan (nave and sanctuary)
Three-cell plan (nave, chancel and sanctuary)
Cruciform plan (nave, transepts, sanctuary and central tower)

A fourth plan type, the Circular, based upon the plan of the Church of the Holy Sepulchre at Jerusalem, was used mainly by the military orders; only five examples have survived (St Sepulchre, Northampton; Temple Church, London; Holy Sepulchre, Cambridge; Little Maplescombe, Essex; Ludlow Castle, Shropshire).

Pre-Conquest churches, surviving due to their construction in stone and to having escaped the transforming zeal of the builders, exist in all three plan types: Escomb, Durham (two-cell plan); Barton-on-Humber, Lincolnshire (three-cell plan); Bradford-on-Avon, Wiltshire (cruciform plan). The pre-Conquest church of Worth in Sussex has, in addition, an apsidal sanctuary, a rare feature in buildings of this date. Larger buildings of this period show a highly developed plan form, worthy of later work. Brixworth in Northamptonshire has an original aisled nave with an arcade of Roman tiles (now filled in with later windows) and an eastern apse above a crypt ambulatory.

The revival of church building which followed the Conquest generally adhered to the two-cell and three-cell plans for the majority of parish churches, either square-ended (Stewkley, Bucks; Adel, Hales, Yorkshire) or apsidal (Kilpeck, Herefordshire; Hales, Norfolk). Sometimes a western tower was provided, sometimes aisles, but rarely both features. The cruciform plan (Old Shoreham, Sussex) had the obvious disadvantage that the massive piers required to support the tower were obstructive and the transept was entirely secluded from

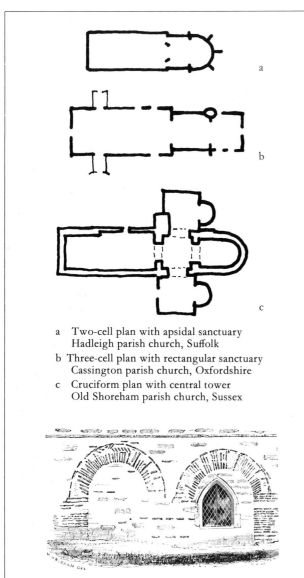

a Two-cell plan with apsidal sanctuary
   Hadleigh parish church, Suffolk
b Three-cell plan with rectangular sanctuary
   Cassington parish church, Oxfordshire
c Cruciform plan with central tower
   Old Shoreham parish church, Sussex

Brixworth Church, Northamptonshire
The arches of the original arcade

the main body of the building. This plan was never generally adopted for parish purposes although later examples were built and have survived (Alfriston, Sussex). Thus it was from the two-cell and three-cell types that the more complex plans of later rebuilding developed: naves have received aisles, clerestories and porches, the chancel has been lengthened or rebuilt, sometimes with aisles and clerestories. New towers have been added, existing ones heightened or replaced. Transepts have merged with aisles, been extended or rebuilt. Chantry chapels have been provided and in some instances magnificent Lady-chapels joined to the original church only by a tenuous link at the east end.

Extensions

All mediaeval extensions were planned to cause as little disturbance as possible to the daily use of the building. With new aisle additions, the external walls were usually constructed first and covered with a new pent roof. The original door was often bodily removed and reconstructed in the new wall (causing later problems of dating). The piers of the arcade were then constructed in gaps cut for the purpose in the original walls, with further breaks formed for the insertion of the voussoirs of the arch. The original wall filling the new arches was then removed and the aisle thrown into the church. Thus it is often found that the walling over the aisle arcade is the oldest portion of the surviving church and the outlines of the original windows are sometimes visible in the masonry.

The construction of a new aisle provided problems of lighting. The simplest solution was to ignore this and continue the slope of the church roof at an unchanged angle, as is commonplace in Sussex churches, for example Wilmington. Sometimes the roof was given a flatter pitch which, while precluding a clerestorey, allowed larger windows to be provided in the comparatively lofty aisle wall (Halifax, Yorkshire). An alternative solution was to gable the aisles at the same height as the nave, a favourite device of fourteenth- and fifteenth-century builders in Devon, Cornwall and Kent (New Romney, Kent).

The simplest solution to the lighting problem was, however, to raise the walls above the arcade and to pierce them with windows. In some early examples a steeply pitched roof was provided but, as most clerestories date from the fifteenth century, a flat-pitched roof provided with parapets was usual, except in Norfolk where the old traditional roof slope was generally retained. Original Norman clerestories survive in a few places (Filey, Yorkshire; Compton Bishop, Somerset). Clerestories became common in the thirteenth century (Darlington, Durham; Hankham, Sussex) and by the fourteenth century were a familiar feature of English parish churches, often having windows enriched with geometrical or curvilinear tracery. In the fifteenth century it was common to find the upper walls presenting an almost unbroken area of coloured glass in the splendid churches of the period (Lavenham and Long Melford, Suffolk; Boston, Lincolnshire; Chipping Norton, Oxfordshire).

The accumulation of chancel chapels was a late development of the English parish church. At first quite small, the number and size increased until they took the form of chancel aisles producing, eventually, a rectangular plan (Old Basing, Hampshire) and resulting in the three-gable east end termination mentioned earlier (Launceston, Cornwall). When aisles and chapels were added to cruciform buildings the original projection of the chancel arms generally constituted a convenient width. The transepts became merged with the general outline of the plan, producing a rectangular form (Odiham, Hampshire). In the fourteenth century the constructional distinction of nave and chancel began to disappear: early chancel arches were rebuilt, enlarged and finally disappeared, being replaced by a wooden rood screen, often of great magnificence. Screens abound in East Anglia (Dennington, Suffolk; Castle Acre, Norfolk) and in some instances stretch across the church from wall to wall (Ippleden, Devon; Old Radnor, Powys).

Below: Long Melford, Suffolk   *Right:* Parish church of St Botolph, Boston, Lincolnshire

Towers

The tall, square western tower was a feature of some pre-Conquest churches (Fingest, Buckinghamshire; Sompting, Sussex). Its primary use was as a belfry but, being built without a staircase and with very small openings in the lower stage, it could be used as a refuge in times of danger. A secondary use for the tower may well have been to provide a dwelling for the parish priest, the provision of an opening looking into the nave from the tower allowing the priest to say night offices without descending to the church (Brixworth, Northamptonshire; Deerhurst, Gloucestershire), with flue and fireplace in the tower to provide heating (Billockby and Thornage, Norfolk).

The west end of the nave was the usual position for the tower in England, and twin towers were built in some places (Melbourne, Derbyshire; St Margaret's, King's Lynn, Norfolk). There are exceptions to general usage, in the shape of flanking towers with the tower stage forming the church porch, found in Norfolk (Little Ellingham; Hardingham) and Cornwall (Veryan; St Stephen-by-Saltash), and transeptal towers in Cornwall (St Patrick, Bodmin), Devon (Ottery St Mary), Dorset (Melbury Bubb) and Sussex (Clymping).

Detached belfries are due to site problems or poor bearing of the subsoil and can be found widely distributed throughout the country. Sometimes they are constructed of stone (West Walton, Norfolk; Long Sutton, Lincolnshire) or of timber (Pembridge, Herefordshire; Brookland, Kent). Such a tower may subsequently be engaged within the fabric of the church, following an extension of the nave aisles. Generally it is then supported on arches (Grantham, Lincolnshire; Milford, Hampshire; St Clements, Hastings, Sussex). Sometimes the tower projects externally but is carried on piers with archways providing passage for processions to make a complete outdoor circuit of the church without leaving consecrated ground (Dedham, Essex; Wrotham, Kent).

In the Eastern counties, where the local flint was often used, the towers of smaller village churches were often circular on plan, resembling the early churches of Ravenna (Bessingham, Norfolk; Southease and Piddinghoe, Sussex). Octagonal upper lanterns are common (Doulting, Somerset) and towers were occasionally built on this plan from the ground (Coxwold, Yorkshire). Octagonal storeys as a transition to a spire are common in Northamptonshire.

Porches

The porch fulfilled two purposes: it provided shelter and protected the door from the weather, and it was used for the performance of portions of the services of baptism, marriage and churching. A pre-Conquest feature emanating from early Christian church

Sompting church tower, Sussex

Lelant, St Ives, Cornwall

architecture of the Mediterranean was the provision of a west porch, or narthex; surviving examples are usually incorporated into the lower storey of the tower (Brixworth, Northamptonshire; Monkswearmouth, Durham). Pre-Conquest south porches have survived (Bishopstone, Sussex) and throughout the Middle Ages porches were provided in this position. A north porch might be provided where the greater part of the village lay on that side (Witney, Oxfordshire). Sometimes a porch was provided on both north and south sides. West porches in post-Conquest churches were rare (Cley, Norfolk; Otford, Kent).

Upper chambers were common by the fourteenth century and can be seen in many East Anglian churches (Eye, Suffolk; St Nicholas, King's Lynn, Norfolk). Some upper chambers contained piscinas (Salle, Norfolk) and were used as occasional chapels. More often they contain fireplaces (Westham, Kent; Northleach, Gloucestershire). The largest and finest example is at Cirencester, Gloucestershire, where the upper floors of the three-storey porch were used by the trade guilds and served for a time as a town hall. The south porch chamber at Grantham, Lincolnshire, was provided with a small projecting window enabling the nightwatchman to command a wide view of the interior. After the Reformation porches were occasionally used as libraries, stores for the parish weapons or schoolrooms.

From the fourteenth century a small rectangular addition was sometimes provided on the north side of the chancel to serve as a sacristy or vestry. Access into the church was by a door in the chancel wall near the high altar (Islip, Northamptonshire; Burford, Oxfordshire). Sometimes such an addition would contain a piscina (Hawton, Nottinghamshire), and it might be of two stories (Chipping Norton, Oxfordshire).

Crypts are rare in parish churches. Pre-Conquest examples survive (Repton, Derbyshire; Wing, Buckinghamshire; Brixworth, Northamptonshire) and later

Kilpeck, Herefordshire
The south door

Newbold-upon-Avon, Warwickshire
The south porch

Parish church of SS. Peter and Paul, Northleach, Gloucestershire

Parish church of St Mary, Rye, Sussex

examples are found generally where the fall of the ground is suitable (Shillington, Bedfordshire; Madley, Herefordshire). When large extensions made to churches in the fifteenth century encroached on the graveyards, charnel houses were constructed under the new buildings to receive the collected remains from the disturbed graves (Chipping Camden, Gloucestershire; Hythe, Kent).

REGIONAL CHARACTERISTICS

Regional characteristics are distinctive in parish church building. These developed from purely practical considerations such as availability of materials, ease of transport, the density of settlement and the economic prosperity of the area. Local varieties of church building may be roughly classified as follows:

1   'Small stone' type of church, usually in remote areas poor in resources. This type is widely and sporadically distributed from the Lincolnshire Wolds to the Welsh borders and from Cumbria to Dorset. Generally built and roofed entirely of local materials (Yelford, Oxfordshire).

2   'Small stoneless' type, prevalent in south-east England, often built of flint and characterised by the little wooden belfry or bellcote over the west gable, with a shingled spirelet (Littlington, Sussex). Timber was used to different degrees, especially in spires (Hemel Hempstead, Hertfordshire), towers (Hurstbourne Tarrant, Hampshire) and porches (Sherborne, Dorset). Brick was used at an early period in Essex due to a dearth of satisfactory alternative materials (Ingatestone; St Osyth).

3   The limestone-belt types from Gloucestershire into Lincolnshire and extending into south-east Yorkshire, where masons produced beautiful examples of their craft from the fine towers of Gloucestershire (Thornbury), the splendid Cotswold perpendicular churches (Cirencester; Northleach; Chipping Camden) and the

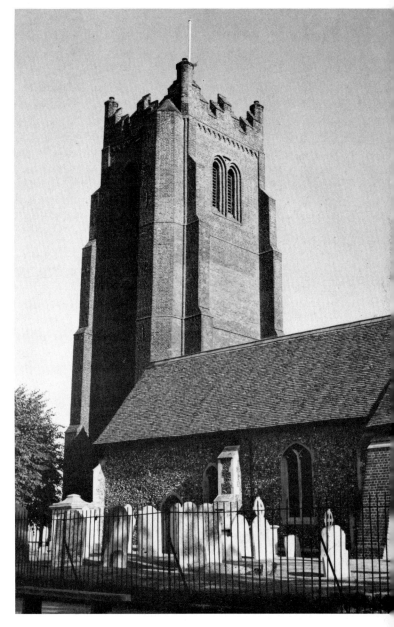

Ingatestone, Essex
The brick tower

Left: Littlington, East Sussex
Below: Parish church of SS. Peter and Paul, Blandford Forum, Dorset

broad spires of Oxfordshire (Witney; Burford) to Northamptonshire (Ketton; Oundle; Kettering) and Lincolnshire (Threckingham).

4   Churches of the south-west with the fine towers of Somerset (Huish Episcopi; Wrington) which tend to overshadow the body of the church, the fine traditions of carved woodwork (Higher Bickington, Devon) and the wagon-vaulted roofs (Launceston and Lelant, Cornwall).

5   The East-Anglian type of Norfolk and Suffolk where, in the fifteenth century, enormous churches were constructed with exteriors of dressed flint often patterned with thin slabs of freestone called flush-work (Southwold, Coddenham and Eye, Suffolk).

6   The churches of the North Midlands where only the great late town churches are outstanding (St Mary, Nottingham; Stafford; Leicester; Chesterfield). In Derbyshire the use of hewn stone slates for roofing led to flattened roofs (Chilmarten), broad spires are common (Baslow), towers are sturdy (Tideswell).

7   Churches of the South Midlands and Welsh borders, where a wide range of geological material has produced no prevailing type. Fine towers and spires occur (Ledbury and Weobley, Herefordshire; Ludlow, Shropshire), characteristic timber belfry tops (Skenfrith, Gwent; Clun, Shropshire) and superlative windows (Ledbury, Ross and All Saints, Hereford). An outstanding feature of this area are the timber towers (Pirton, Worcestershire) and whole fabrics (Nether Peover, Cheshire).

8   Churches of the north where, apart from Yorkshire, much has been obliterated by restoration. Fine later-developing mediaeval communities produced fine Yorkshire churches (Thirsk; Rotherham; Kirk Sandal). The average Yorkshire church is long and low, with a flattened roof for stone slates, and square windows. Battlemented parapets are common, with thin pinacles (Halifax), and there is a fine tower-building tradition, especially in the West Riding

St Peter Mancroft, Norwich, Norfolk

Clun, Shropshire
The tower

Below: Parish church of St Peter, Ludlow, Shropshire
Right: Halifax, Yorkshire, the tower

(Cottingham, Tickhill, Halifax). Many of these towers are provided with open parapet-work in a local idiom.

Church building came almost to an end in the years immediately after 1535, and during the reign of Elizabeth I there was probably less church building than in any

half-century since the Conquest. Apart from a few isolated examples (Woodham Walter, Essex) the Elizabethan contribution was mainly confined to fittings, tombs and memorial plaques. The situation did not improve much during the first half of the seventeenth century, the only new church of note being that of St John, Leeds, Yorkshire. A number of older churches were rebuilt (Bletchley, Buckinghamshire; St Nicholas, Rochester, Kent), reflecting poor classical detail but internally embellished by their hammerbeam roofs, screens and pulpits. One or two ecclesiastical buildings are of note, St Paul's, Covent Garden, and the Queen's Chapel, St James's Palace, London, being outstanding examples of the genius of Inigo Jones.

The revolution in church design which marked the closing years of the seventeenth century was due mainly to the work of Sir Christopher Wren, whose London churches rising from the ashes of the Great Fire of 1666 created a new spatial and decorative concept in the High Renaissance style, designed for Protestant worship and preaching. Fifty-two city churches were rebuilt under his direction, including St Clement Danes, St James, Piccadilly, and St Anne Soho.

Following the work of Wren in the City of London came the churches constructed under the Act of 1711 for the building of fifty new churches in or near the Cities of London and Westminster or their suburbs. Several architects were involved in this ambitious scheme: James Gibbs was responsible for St Mary-le-Strand, St Martin-in-the-Fields and St Peter, Vere Street; Thomas Archer for St Paul, Deptford and St John, Smith Square; Nicholas Hawksmoor for St Anne, Limehouse, St Mary Woolnoth and St George, Bloomsbury, among others. All were designed incorporating classical motifs, many with galleries and all of exceptional quality.

During this period a number of charming country parish churches were built under the classical influence (King Charles the Martyr, Tunbridge Wells, Kent; St Mary, Blandford, Dorset, designed by John and William Bastard; Glynde, Sussex; Mereworth, Kent, designed by Colin Campbell). All are buildings of quality and most are worthy additions to ecclesiastical architecture. The former chapel of Great Witney Court, Worcestershire, now the parish church, is a treasure-house of craftsmanship and colour.

The Gothic style in church building had never completely died out but continued to be used where occasion warranted. A good example is the use by Hawksmoor of a Gothic style incorporating bastard classical motifs in the twin western towers of Westminster Abbey. Many Gothic restorations were carried out in the eighteenth century, and a few complete rebuildings (Tetbury, Worcestershire; St Nicholas, Warwick).

It was not until the Church Building Act of 1818 that church building once more became common and of the 214 churches erected as a result of this Act, 174 were in the Gothic style. Some of these deserve attention (St Luke, Chelsea, London; East Grinstead, Sussex; St Peter, Brighton, Sussex) but many are visually weak in construction and the detailing is usually poor. Later work of the nineteenth century improved under the scholarship of J. L. Pearson (St Augustine, Kilburn, London), Gilbert Scott (St Mary Abbott, Kensington, London) and G. E. Street (St Saviour, Eastbourne, Sussex). The great majority of Gothic revival work was, however, poor and mean, a travesty of the original inspiration; sterile; dead.

With Gothic revival came Gothic restoration, when parish churches without number were stripped and gutted of their accumulated beauties of the past three centuries under the cloak of mediaevalism. The destruction of this period probably was exceeded only by the dismantling of the conventual houses in the sixteenth century, and was made worse in that it was carried out by men of culture and intelligence and not merely by ignorant breakers consumed by greed and political bias.

Below : Parish church of St Martin-in-the-Fields, Trafalgar Square, London

Right : Parish church of St Swithun, East Grinstead, Sussex

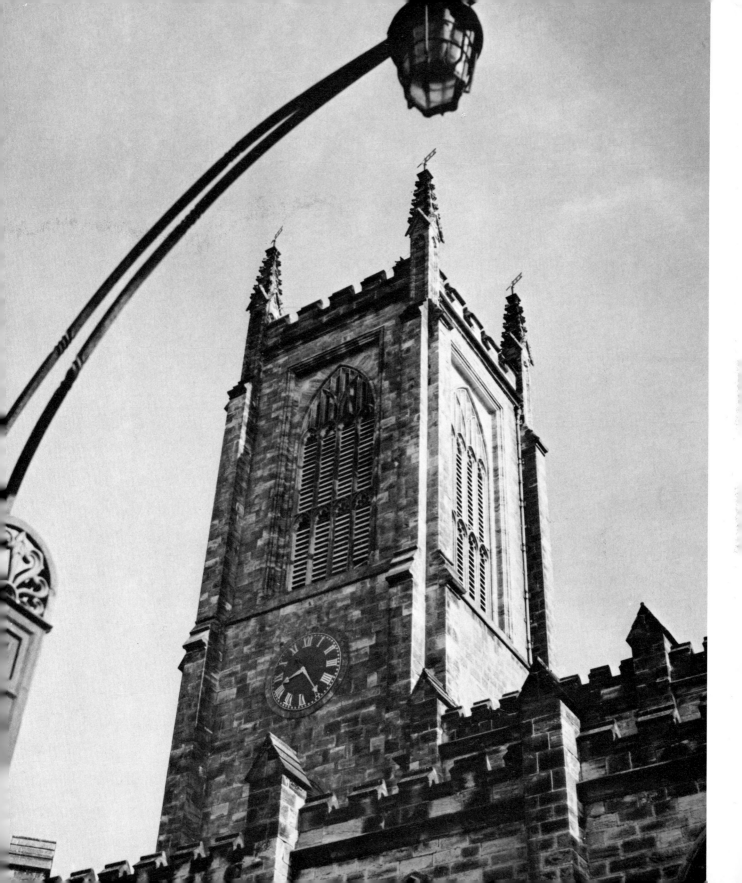

Chapter Four

The Construction of Churches

The structural elements of a church, as of all buildings, comprise support, roofing, abutment and lighting. Their evolution and development form the basic ingredients of all architectural design and must be considered closely in any study of building types. The proportions of the design were often dictated by the structural limitations of both materials and builders and, while increased skills and better knowledge led to lighter and higher constructions, certain features were still provided which, like the splendid towers of so many cathedral churches (Gloucester; York), owed much more to dramatic architectural effect than to purely structural considerations.

VAULTING

All building is subservient to the erection and maintenance of a protective covering over planned space; Gothic architecture was no exception. Mediaeval builders covered most of the greater churches with stone ceilings to reduce as far as possible the risk of fire from the roof, stone vaults providing an effective barrier (Norwich Cathedral, Norfolk). This stone vault was an expensive item, only to be provided in important and wealthy foundations. Even many of these latter, however, found the cost of a stone vault prohibitive and vaults of wood resembling stone forms are sometimes found (York Minster). Stone vaults were not proof against the weather and needed a timber roof with a weatherproof covering to keep out the elements. These roofs were often covered with thatch or oak shingles until money was available for lead or tiles (Salisbury Cathedral, Wiltshire). All vault construction strove to reduce the weight of the structure by economy in the quantity of material used and to minimise the amount of supporting timberwork (centering) used in the construction (St John's, Tower of London).

The oldest and simplest vault is the 'barrel' and its intersection in aisle bays produces the groined vault

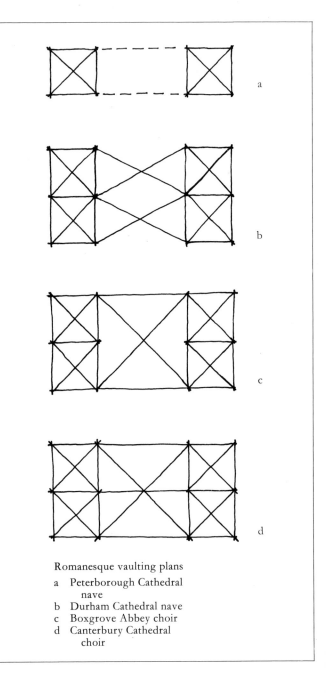

Romanesque vaulting plans
a   Peterborough Cathedral
   nave
b   Durham Cathedral nave
c   Boxgrove Abbey choir
d   Canterbury Cathedral
   choir

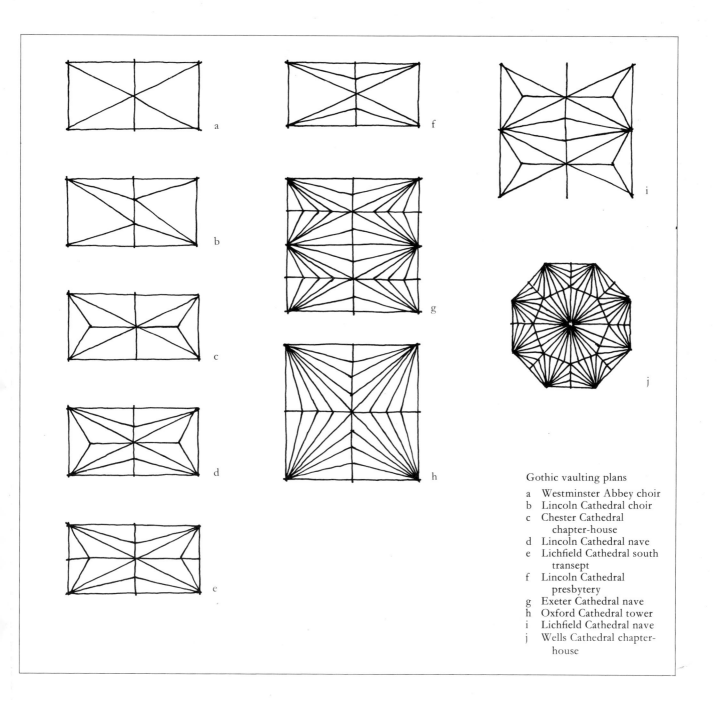

Gothic vaulting plans

a Westminster Abbey choir
b Lincoln Cathedral choir
c Chester Cathedral
     chapter-house
d Lincoln Cathedral nave
e Lichfield Cathedral south
     transept
f Lincoln Cathedral
     presbytery
g Exeter Cathedral nave
h Oxford Cathedral tower
i Lichfield Cathedral nave
j Wells Cathedral chapter-
     house

Kirkstead Chapel, Lincolnshire

(Norwich Cathedral). This vault is both heavy and expensive as it requires to be constructed as a homogeneous mass on a continuous platform or shuttering. To increase the strength of the groined vault, a transverse arch was sometimes constructed (Gloucester Cathedral), but this form of vaulting was not satisfactory or practical for covering the high, wide naves of the earlier great churches, most of which were roofed and ceiled in wood (Peterborough Cathedral, Cambridgeshire).

The greatest step forward in vault construction was undoubtedly the introduction of the arch rib, which may be regarded as permanent stone centering. This rib was erected first, substituting strong arches for the weak edges of the groined vault, the voids being filled in later with ashlar, rubble or chalk. The earliest rib stone vault was erected at Durham Cathedral, the work commencing in 1093. Two geometrical problems faced the masons: first, that of vaulting a rectangular space, and, second, the shape of the rib arches. The first problem was solved at Boxgrove Priory in Sussex by the introduction

of a large square bay to the nave, corresponding to two smaller square bays in the aisles, and the second by the introduction of the pointed arch, which had an immediate effect on the whole technique of vaulting. This, then, formed the basis of quadripartite vaulting with two diagonal and usually two transverse ribs (Peterborough Cathedral; Abbey Dore, Herefordshire). Vaulting developed by the addition of a centre ridge rib and transverse ridge ribs, with wall ribs to define the edges of each compartment (Gloucester Cathedral).

Most English vaults were low in height compared with French examples; this caused a problem, not only aesthetically, in that the vault appeared to press down on the arcades like a lid, but also practically, in preserving the efficiency of the clerestorey windows. To overcome the problem the vaulting was turned back into the reveals of the windows to produce the ploughshare vault (Pershore Abbey, Worcestershire; Southwark Cathedral, London). Where a number of vaulting ribs converged on a shaft it was usual to form these from a single stone built into the wall in the form of a corbel, providing a feature of immense strength (Lichfield Cathedral, Staffordshire). Where the ribs intersected at the crown of the vault it was often the practice to provide a boss, often of great size and usually carved with scenes from the Scriptures or with other ecclesiastical features (Chester Cathedral; Westminster Abbey). Although these carvings are too high above the floor to be seen clearly they are, in fact, executed with the same care and skill as carved work at floor level.

Pursuing their vaulting experiments, English builders introduced transverse ribs called tiercerons which, subdividing the planes of the vault, eased constructional problems and improved appearance while increasing strength (Great Malvern Priory, Worcestershire). This developed into the lierne vault with subsidiary ribs connecting the main ribs as ties, serving no other purpose but decoration. Carried a step further, this became known as the stellar pattern and was common in

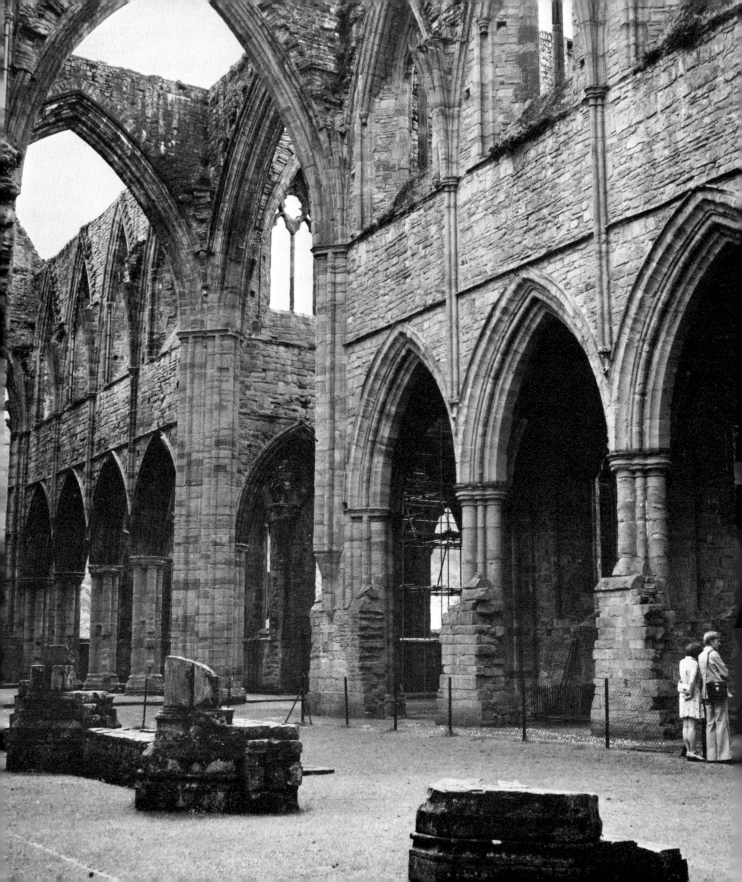

Sherborne Minster, Dorset,
the nave vaulting

later vaults (Tewkesbury Abbey, Gloucestershire). Its flexibility of application allowed any unusual shape or irregular plan to be vaulted with ease. Polygonal chapter-houses (Westminster Abbey; Lichfield and Wells Cathedrals) were vaulted in this way from a central pier.

From the stellar vault came the exclusively English vault form known as fan vaulting, with ribs spreading out in the shape of a fan or palm to form an inverted trumpet (Oxford Cathedral; Henry VII Chapel, Westminster Abbey; King's College Chapel, Cambridge; Bath and Sherborne Abbeys). The fan vault originated at Gloucester Cathedral in the east cloister walk, c. 1375. It is constructed of strong arches spanning the compartment, partially concealed, with the rib and filling replaced by an arched wagon vault of which the members are cut from one and the same stone; the surface of this is patterned with pendants from which fans spread out to meet each other.

TIMBER ROOFS

The wooden roofs which covered the vaults were generally fine examples of straightforward carpentry. The only example of a decorative structural roof in a major church is the hammerbeam roof in the transepts at Ely Cathedral, Cambridgeshire, although many parish churches now raised to cathedral status exhibit fine examples of the carpenter's art. While a few parish churches have stone vaulting, usually in the apsidal east ends and chancels (Elkstone, Gloucestershire), the usual form of roof was of timber; many fine examples survive to the present day (Bocking, Essex; Adderbury, Oxfordshire).

The development of the mediaeval timber roof of the smaller church, as distinct from the buildings of the monastic foundations, may be said to have begun with open-rafter construction. No tie-beams were provided or needed to tie in the sturdy stone walls of these buildings. As the buildings grew in width and size so the

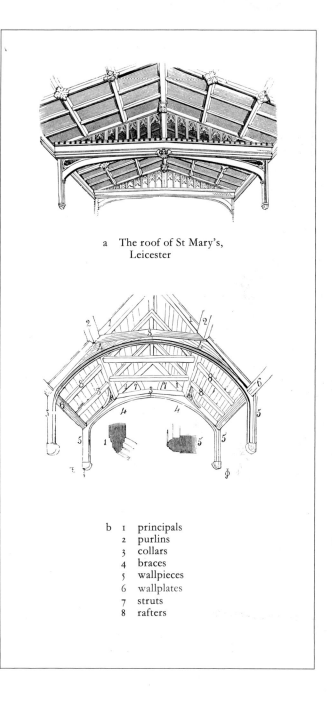

a   The roof of St Mary's,
Leicester

b   1   principals
2   purlins
3   collars
4   braces
5   wallpieces
6   wallplates
7   struts
8   rafters

Parish church of SS. Peter and Paul, Salle, Norfolk
Open-rafter construction

thrust upon the outside walls from the rafters also grew, and a device known as the scissor truss was employed as a means to help arrest the spread of the rafters at plate level.

This form of roof construction quickly changed in the early part of the thirteenth century, although examples are to be found down to the end of the period of church building. A type which included the tie-beam became the order of the day. These ties, both in the aisled church and in the building consisting only of nave and chancel, were placed at regular intervals; where arcades between nave and aisle occurred, the ties were placed approximately above the columns, thus tying in the walls in the most satisfactory manner possible.

From the end of each tie, wall plates were secured. In the aisled building they were three in number, and in the non-aisled building two were employed, linked together with bridging pieces. From these plates rose the rafters, and the ashlars which were introduced as a further means of securing the feet of the rafters. At a point approximately one-third of the way down from the apex of each rafter a collar was tennoned, and from the centre of the tie-beam a slender column rose (a feature introduced from western France). This, in turn, quickly gave rise to the use of a horizontal member from one end of the building to the other, placed immediately under the collars and known as the collar purlin, to which the timber column was attached. A little later still, braces were introduced from each collar to the rafter. Thus the whole roof became one of sturdy equilibrium. The central column now became increased in girth and from each side of its square-faced head sprang brackets fixed to the collar purlin and the braces of the rafters immediately above it. Below this the column was reduced to the section of an octagon with shaped and moulded cap and base.

Known as crown-post construction, this system continued as the mode for the next three centuries. However, although the common form of construction,

particularly in the south-east of the country, it was by no means the only one in use. In the west of England the tie-beam seems to have received less honour than elsewhere; the rafters were often covered in, with additional members cut to form and plaster or boarding used as a means to complete either a barrel vault or waggon roof, divided into square compartments with carved bosses at the intersections (Lelant, Cornwall). Often a still further type of construction was employed, consisting of a heavy timber arch built up from sections and rising from corbels, and supporting a large tie at its apex, which in turn supported heavy moulded purlins to which the ordinary rafters were attached. This form became known as the arched braced truss or collar-braced type.

It is from this form rather than from any other that the hammerbeam roof developed, when exceptionally large spaces could be spanned only by building up in sections, with each section forming part of the ingenious whole. Many examples exist in a variety of forms, including the great roof of Westminster Hall and one style found particularly in East Anglia. The double hammerbeam roof (March, Cambridgeshire), often provided with carved and gilded angels, is one of the glories of English carpentry. Variations of all types occur,

Part of the roof of Adderbury Church, Oxfordshire

A tie-beam
B king post
C principal
D strut
E brace
F wallpiece
G longitudinal strut
H ridgepiece

sometimes one type of roof alternated with another in adjoining bays (Necton, Norfolk).

Two later examples of roof construction utilised the growing preference for lead sheet to weather roofs. In the first type, where the rafters were only a short distance above the tie-beam, the triangular space was filled in with wooden tracery, sometimes combined with a king or queen post. This style was common in Somerset and Devon (St Cuthbert, Wells, Somerset). The second provided for a cambered tie-beam with the purlins and rafters resting directly on it, the ends of the tie being supported by carved arch-braces brought well down the walls and supported on stone corbels (Lavenham, Suffolk). Post-Reformation church roofs often incorporated hammerbeam construction (South Harting, Sussex) but after the Restoration most Renaissance churches were provided with fine plaster ceilings (St Charles the Martyr, Tunbridge Wells, Kent).

Roofs require a supporting structure and this was provided by a complex system of walls, piers, arches and buttresses which developed from simple massive elements to graceful symphonies in stone. These structures were designed on an empirical basis, mostly with complete success, although there are many cases of towers and spires which collapsed with disastrous results (Ely Cathedral tower, Durham choir vault).

WALLS AND BUTTRESSES

Romanesque wall construction was massive but weak, generally comprising two skins of dressed stone with the intervening void filled with rubble and stone chippings roughly set in lime mortar. This core tended to remain weak due to lack of the carbon dioxide necessary to complete the chemical reaction to produce hard mortar; in many buildings the core shrank away from the encasing dressed stone, leaving this to carry the main weight of the structure. These walls were satisfactory

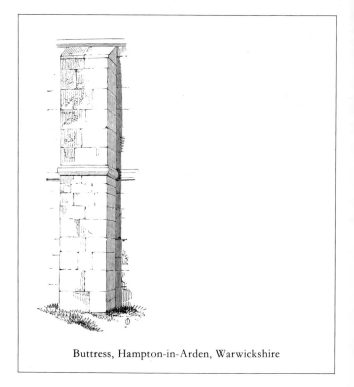

Buttress, Hampton-in-Arden, Warwickshire

when timber or simple barrel and groined vaults were used, the structural bay being defined by a flat rectangular buttress, more aesthetic than useful.

With the construction of ribbed vaults and the use of thin ashlar walls, the buttress became indispensable. Initially provided by a rectangular mass of stone surmounted by a tall, sloping top (Kirkstall Abbey, Yorkshire), this developed into the tall pillar buttress with two or more offsets to weather the setback as the thickness of the buttress was reduced (Lichfield Cathedral Lady-chapel, Staffordshire). These buttresses were refined until, by the fourteenth century, when the size of windows expanded virtually to fill the space between them, buttresses fulfilled completely the original function of the wall to sustain the weight and thrust of the vault and safely transmit the thrust to the foundations

Buttress, St Lawrence's,
Evesham, Worcestershire

Pier at Norwich Cathedral

(St Mary Redcliffe, Bristol, Avon). Masons soon discovered that it was vital to weigh down the top of the buttress to ensure the stability of the masonry and, from being merely a decorative feature of Romanesque design (St David's Cathedral, Dyfed), the pinnacle, in a variety of forms and decorative appearance, became the formal termination of a buttress (Winchester Cathedral, Hampshire).

To counteract the thrust of the high vaults and at the same time keep the height of the aisles to a reasonable level, an arch segment was constructed between the top of the buttress and the thrust line of the vault where this impinged on the upper wall of the clerestorey (Lincoln Cathedral). It was soon discovered that this arch, or flying buttress, must be set at an acute angle with the arch of the vault rib, describing as complete a semi-circle as possible.

In some instances the later churches of the fourteenth century and early fifteenth century required flying buttresses in series (Malmesbury Abbey, Wiltshire; Bath Abbey, Avon). The most prolific use of flying buttresses is at Westminster Abbey where French influence produced a church comparable in height with those of the Ile de France and requiring serried ranks of flying buttresses to withstand the thrust. All this expenditure of material and energy became redundant when the aisles were raised to an equal height with the nave (Bristol Cathedral, Avon), so that the thrusts from the vaults were equal and opposed and so cancelled one another.

THE STRUCTURAL BAY

The interior of the church is designed around the bay with, in most cases, its division into arcade, triforium and clerestorey. This changed from a massive solidity to an airy graciousness as more knowledge and skill were utilised in its construction and the elements were composed in varying proportions. In the majority of Romanesque churches the three compartments are practically equal in height and the effect is to make the

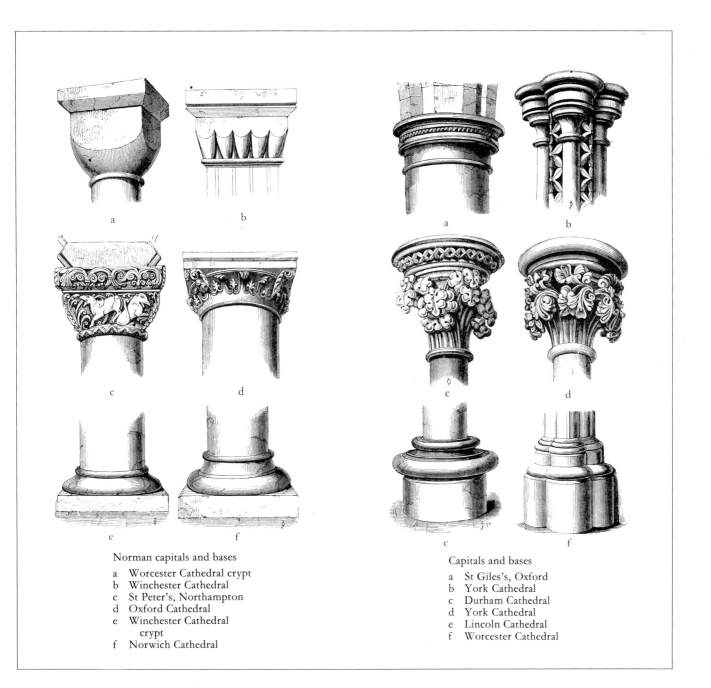

Norman capitals and bases

a   Worcester Cathedral crypt
b   Winchester Cathedral
c   St Peter's, Northampton
d   Oxford Cathedral
e   Winchester Cathedral
    crypt
f   Norwich Cathedral

Capitals and bases

a   St Giles's, Oxford
b   York Cathedral
c   Durham Cathedral
d   York Cathedral
e   Lincoln Cathedral
f   Worcester Cathedral

a   Stanton Harcourt,
     Oxfordshire
b   Salisbury Cathedral

arcade squat, dwarfed by the burden of the structure it carries (Leominster, Herefordshire). The later work at Durham Cathedral is better proportioned and the improvement can also be seen at Chichester Cathedral, Sussex, and Christchurch Priory in Hampshire. Sometimes the piers alternate between massive cylinders and sculptured rectangles with vaulting shafts rising from the floor to the crown of the vault (Durham Cathedral). Above the arcade, the Romanesque triforium is usually composed of two arches springing from a central column, the whole enclosed in an all-embracing arch (Southwell Minster, Nottinghamshire). The piers of the arcade and the supporting walls of clerestorey and triforium were usually constructed of rubble-filled masonary.

The introduction of the pointed arch and its development in the thirteenth century produced three types of triforium: a Gothic version of the Romanesque two-arch unit (Lincoln Cathedral choir), a form of continuous lancet arcading of great simplicity (Wells Cathedral nave, Somerset) and a more intricate interlacing of motifs (Beverley Minster, Yorkshire). At Ripon Cathedral, Yorkshire, the triforium bay is formed of four lancets, the central pair being divided by a spandrel pierced with quatrefoil. The clerestorey of this period usually follows the triforium design, generally, however, reduced in height, sometimes designed as a single lancet with small attendant blank arches on either side (Ripon Cathedral choir).

With the introduction of geometrical tracery the design of the bay increased in richness, the effect depending much on the relative proportions. At Westminster Abbey the bay design was of great height and narrow in width, while at Lincoln Cathedral the high bay was of exceptional width. These two examples illustrate the diversity of approach. The Angel Choir at Lincoln is perhaps the most perfect example of high Gothic art, with its triforium comprising two pointed arches, each incorporating a trefoil-headed arch, the spandrel above moulded and pierced with a richly moulded quatrefoil,

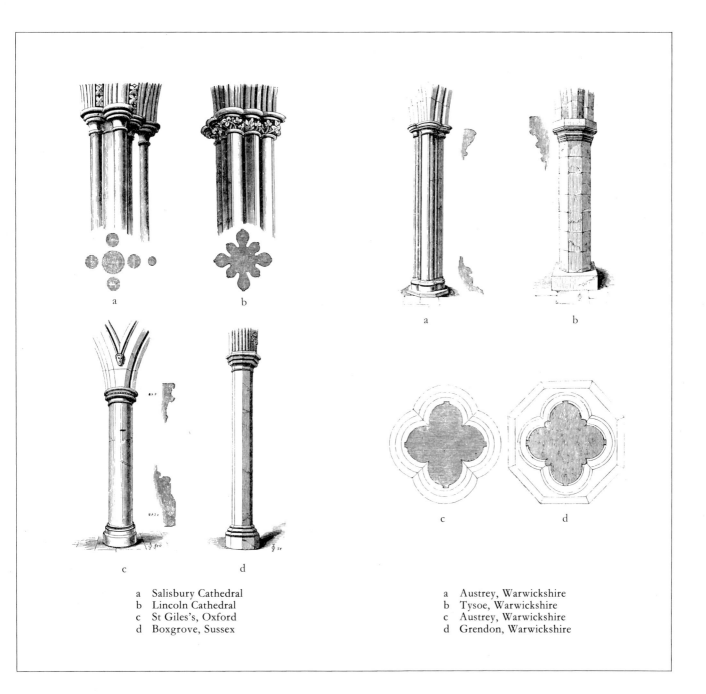

a   Salisbury Cathedral
b   Lincoln Cathedral
c   St Giles's, Oxford
d   Boxgrove, Sussex

a   Austrey, Warwickshire
b   Tysoe, Warwickshire
c   Austrey, Warwickshire
d   Grendon, Warwickshire

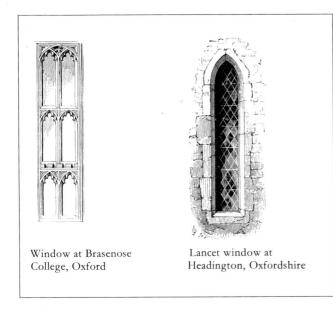

Window at Brasenose
College, Oxford

Lancet window at
Headington, Oxfordshire

Norman windows

a   Gillingham, Norfolk
b   Ryton, Warwickshire
c   Beaudesert, Warwickshire

and the clerestorey with its four trefoil-headed windows and elaborate traceried infilling in the arch above.

In the fourteenth century the triforium as a separate element died out except for a band of blind arcading dividing the main arcade from the clerestorey (Winchester Cathedral nave, Hampshire). The finest example is to be found in the remodelling of Gloucester Cathedral choir, where the masons ignored the proportions of the Romanesque structure and faced up the whole with an airy framework of stone mullions and light panelling which soars from floor to vaulting-bosses. At York Minster the finely proportioned arcade is provided with a well-designed clerestorey window surmounting a band of openwork panelling which disguises the triforium passage.

WINDOWS AND TRACERY

Artificial lighting in churches was almost non-existent. They relied solely on candles, either singly or in groups on iron candelabra (Rowlstone, Herefordshire) or stone cressets, of which an example survives at Brecon Cathedral, Powys. It was therefore necessary at all times to admit as much natural daylight to the building as possible. The size of windows was restricted by problems of thrust and structural stability which required, in Romanesque construction, the maximum amount of solid masonry between buttresses and the spring of ribbed vaults or the

Ely Cathedral, Cambridgeshire
The lantern

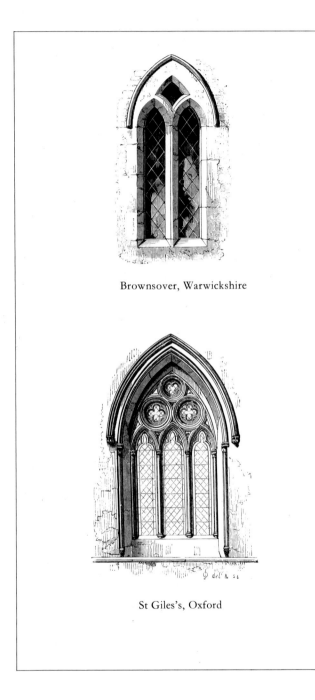

Brownsover, Warwickshire

St Giles's, Oxford

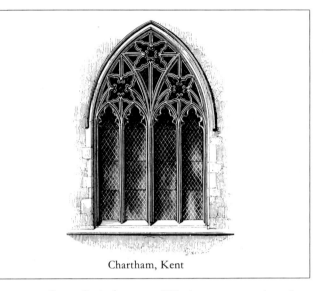

Chartham, Kent

centres of roof tie-beams. Windows were therefore restricted to small round-headed lights with deeply splayed internal reveals (West Dean, East Sussex).

With the solving of the problems of abutment, windows in the twelfth century began to match the pointed arches of the arcades. These windows, generally referred to as lancets, took contrasting forms. The North Country school of masons favoured tall, narrow windows (Hexham Abbey, Northumberland), while at Canterbury and in the West Country the masons favoured a shorter, wider proportion (Wells Cathedral, Somerset; Pershore Abbey, Worcestershire). Tall, narrow lancet windows were soon grouped in threes with a taller central light (Lincoln Cathedral nave) which greatly increased the quality of the elevational design. At York Minster, the north transept is lit by two tiers, each of five lancets, the lowest of uniform height rising through two stories and known as the 'Five Sisters', surmounted by five small graded lancets in the gable.

The way was now clear for the introduction of big multi-light traceried gable windows. Side lighting was obtained through aisle windows and also clerestory

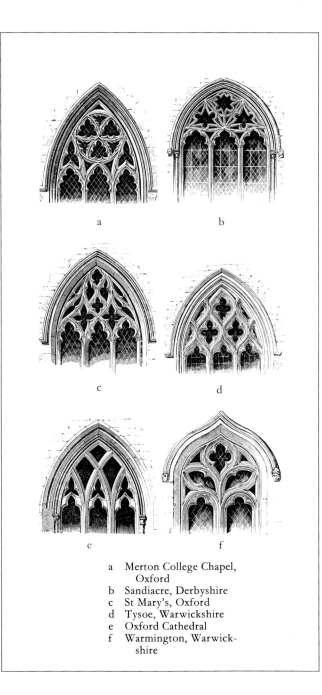

a   Merton College Chapel,
      Oxford
b   Sandiacre, Derbyshire
c   St Mary's, Oxford
d   Tysoe, Warwickshire
e   Oxford Cathedral
f   Warmington, Warwick-
      shire

windows in the larger churches (Rye, Sussex). These windows were enlarged and developed until they ultimately reduced the triforium to a decorative band (Gloucester Cathedral choir). In some cases, however, the aisle windows were given extra prominence, resulting in diminished size and importance for the clerestorey (Tewkesbury Abbey, Gloucestershire). A compromise is found in several examples, notably at Ely Cathedral, where a further range of windows was provided above those lighting the aisles to provide illumination for the triforium, enabling this to be used for ecclesiastical purposes. The cost of raising the aisle walls and the restricting influence this had on the design of the triforium arcades made this an unpopular feature and the fashion had died out before the middle of the fourteenth century.

The grouping of lancets under a common dripstone at Romsey Abbey, Hampshire, with the spandrels left solid, was probably the first move in England towards traceried windows. It was a short step to pierce the spandrel (Binham Priory, Norfolk), leading to the development of the large multi-light window strengthened with vertical stone mullions and with decorative tracery at the head. The first phase was known as 'geometrical' when plate or pierced tracery was replaced by bar tracery formed of separate stones, usually in the form of cusped circles (Tintern Abbey, Gwent). Later, by the end of the thirteenth century, quatrefoil and cinquefoil work came into use, often incorporated in a circular centrepiece (Chester Cathedral choir). A feature of this period was the incorporation of ball flower ornament around the windows (Leominster Priory, Herefordshire).

Circular windows filled with tracery were popular in the twelfth century (Peterborough Cathedral), and developed into the beautiful rose windows which are such a feature of the transepts of many greater churches (Lincoln Cathedral; York Minster; Westminster Abbey). By the fourteenth century designers had tired of precise

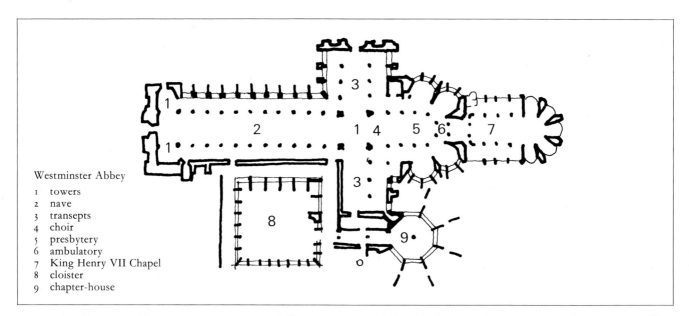

Westminster Abbey

1 towers
2 nave
3 transepts
4 choir
5 presbytery
6 ambulatory
7 King Henry VII Chapel
8 cloister
9 chapter-house

geometrical forms and began to experiment with flowing curves which depended on the intricacy and beauty of arrangement of stone tracery for their effect (York Minster; Beverley Minster; Exeter Cathedral). A variation of this form was the 'reticulated', where the whole window head was filled with cusped ovals (Westminster Abbey, Great Cloister arcade).

Curvilinear tracery died out in the years following the Black Death, being replaced by a simpler rectilinear or perpendicular form which gave full reign to the artistic achievements of the glazier's craft. As the fifteenth century progressed, the pointed arch became flattened until it developed into the four-centre Tudor arch which can best be seen at St George's Chapel, Windsor. In the West Country at Gloucester Cathedral, in the great churches of the Cotswolds (Chipping Camden, Gloucestershire) and in those of East Anglia (Lavenham and Long Melford, Suffolk; Terrington St Clement, Norfolk) can be seen the finest achievements of a style which lasted longer than any previous expression of Gothic building, representing the ideal of natural lighting coupled with the growing taste for coloured glass. The ultimate was achieved in the sixteenth-century royal chapels of St George, Windsor, King's College, Cambridge, and Henry VII at Westminster.

The work of the thirteenth-century glazier, where lancet windows and deepset reveals posed problems of daylighting, was generally in the form of patterned windows called 'grisailles', provided with little colour that appeared in wreaths of foliage and the narrow surrounding bands. The decoration was obtained by painted outlines, hatching and leadwork, sometimes enriched by medallions (York Minster, the Five Sisters window and the chapter-house). Where natural lighting was not of such importance, the work of this period was highly coloured in reds, blues, greens, mauves and white, with designs built up from a large number of small pieces. The lives of the saints, from the Old and New Testaments, were depicted in round or square compartments fitted into a wrought iron frame. The wealth of glass from the *ateliers* of Chartres reached its zenith in the early part of the thirteenth century, and the

King's College Chapel, Cambridge

Long Itchington, Warwickshire

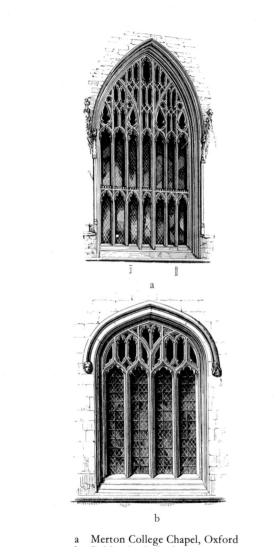

a   Merton College Chapel, Oxford
b   St Mary's, Oxford

windows of Canterbury Cathedral are the finest examples to be found in England. With the introduction of traceried windows drawing became more pictorial, heraldic shields and the figures of donors being commonly depicted. The introduction of a yellow stain, obtained by adding silver to the composition of the glass, provided a range of lighter colours which can be seen in many fine examples at York Minster and Tewkesbury Abbey, Gloucestershire.

With the introduction of Perpendicular tracery in the fifteenth century came the employment of great areas of white glass framing coloured figures, singly or in groups, many in architectural settings under canopies or set in niches. Drawing and painting was of superlative quality and the windows often of great size. The east window of Gloucester Cathedral, commemorating the battle of Crècy, measures 72 foot by 38 foot; the similar window at York Minster, only slightly smaller, incorporates 117 biblical scenes from the Creation to the Apocalypse.

So little of the finest achievement of the English artist has survived the hand of the despoiler that only by comparing the beauty of surviving examples with the dead and lifeless seventeenth-century white glass at Halifax can the true loss be appreciated.

THE TOWER

As an architectural feature, the tower was a culmination of English Gothic achievement. Tower-building, generally, developed fairly late, when the art of bellringing became popular. It was realised, however, that one or more lofty and well-proportioned towers were an aesthetic improvement to most churches. Surviving Norman towers are generally squat, as so many of the higher ones collapsed soon after construction (Romsey Abbey, Hampshire), but enough survive to exhibit the profuse ornamentation which is characteristic of the Romanesque tower (Norwich Cathedral; Tewkesbury Abbey).

The thirteenth century was not a great period for tower-building, except for New Shoreham, Sussex, and the two towers flanking the west front at Peterborough Cathedral. The end of this century and the beginning of the fourteenth marked a great period of tower construction, remarkable for the accentuated verticality of the designs (Lincoln Cathedral; Hereford Cathedral; Salisbury Cathedral), culminating in the twin western towers of York Minster. The climax came in the next one hundred years with a series of lofty constructions of superb quality. Among the great churches, Durham, Worcester and Gloucester Cathedrals, with Great Malvern Priory and the parish churches of Evesham, Worcestershire, Bridgnorth, Shropshire, and Long Melford, Suffolk, are all of equal quality.

Many towers were once surmounted by spires but most have disappeared over the years. Those which survive owe this to continual renovation and repairs to both stonework and foundations. Notable among those which in recent years have required strengthening are Norwich and Salisbury Cathedrals. Stone spires on parish churches are more numerous, especially in the limestone belt of the Midlands (Ketton, Leicestershire; Higham Ferrers, Northamptonshire), but many oak-framed spires covered with shingles or lead survive. The loftiest of these is at Chesterfield, Derbyshire, incorporating the famous twist; numerous low spirelets surmount the towers of Sussex village churches, giving them a lowly charm and grace (Wilmington, Sussex).

Salisbury Cathedral, Wiltshire
The spire

Chapter Five

Nonconformist
Chapels
and
Meeting Houses

Top: Norwich, Norfolk, the Octagon Chapel
Bottom: Tewkesbury, Gloucestershire, Baptist Old Meeting House

Nonconformity has been part of the religious life of the British Isles for over 300 years. It is a matter for some concern that the architectural heritage which belongs to Nonconformists of all communities and the importance of these buildings in the landscape are so little appreciated. Most English and Welsh communities have their 'Zion' or 'Bethel' and some have several. Usually built by local labour with funds raised from the least affluent members of the community, they remain ignored by architectural historians and compilers of guide-books. Where early buildings survive, this is more often due to chance; prosperity has done more damage than neglect—many fine buildings have been replaced by new as congregations enlarged. The conversion of the small vernacular chapel into a cottage or petrol station is a common occurrence.

Although many early chapels showed a degree of rejection of religious symbolism such as the steeple and a need to provide a preaching-house rather than a home for priestly ritual, some of the earliest exhibit sophisticated architecture of the very finest order. Examples are the Octagon chapel at Norwich, Norfolk, and the Friar Street chapel at Ipswich, Suffolk, both of which were built by prosperous communities well acquainted with the latest architectural fashions.

In country districts vernacular examples abound. The Congregational chapel at Walpole in Suffolk was converted from two cottages and its furniture and fittings are delightful examples of real craftsmanship. At Horningsham in Wiltshire (dated 1566) the thatched roof is still intact. These two chapels exemplify the great proportion of surviving early buildings, well built in the local idiom and finished with homely benches and tables.

For centuries the church was the centre of village life and the focal point of the village plan. Chapels, on the other hand, rarely occupy a prominent position, except in industrial towns. Many are the result of an early history of secret meetings on moorlands and in fields and are situated on lonely roads, miles from a possible

Bury St Edmunds, Suffolk
Ex-Unitarian Chapel

Norwich, Norfolk
Congregational 'Old Meeting'

Above: Lyme Regis, Dorset, United Reformed Church
Left: Bridgnorth, Shropshire, United Reformed Methodist Chapel

Brighton Unitarian Church, Sussex

congregation. Hay Lane chapel between Swindon and Wooton Bassett, Wiltshire, and Maesroenan chapel near Glasbury in Powys, are typical examples. Others are on the outskirts of villages or in quiet back streets, as is the finely proportioned Baptist chapel in Stow-on-the-Wold, Gloucestershire. Occasionally the chapel achieves a status similar to that of the church, complete with large graveyard, but still it is usually to be found on the outskirts of the town (New Mill Baptist, Tring, Hertfordshire).

Apart from a few isolated examples, usually to be found in urban areas, most nineteenth-century chapels are in the vernacular tradition, using local materials. Towards the end of the century, larger and sometimes spectacularly vulgar buildings appeared in the towns, ending the recognisable tradition of chapel design. The essential features of the early chapels were a rectangular structure with a gable end to the roof, incorporating a door or doors, windows and usually a plaque. These elevations were invariably symmetrical and gave onto a forecourt; as time passed, a porch, flights of steps and other features were added.

By the end of the nineteenth century the elevation would be covered with a wealth of ornament and the steps and porch had become a dominant architectural feature. The floor of the chapel was often raised well above ground level, the space below being used as a Sunday School hall. Roofs were usually gabled, but in the eastern counties hips following local traditions were normal. Materials used generally followed local traditions and it was only in industrial areas or towards the end of the nineteenth century that engineering bricks of glaring red became the accepted material for chapel construction. Classical forms were early adopted, probably in reaction against the current arguments for Gothic as a building style for churches. Many of the surviving examples are of great beauty: fine examples are the Wesleyan chapel at Louth, Lincolnshire, and Brighton Unitarian Church, Sussex.

Above: Maesroenan Congregational Chapel, Glasbury, Powys
Right: Bridport, Dorset, the Friends' Meeting House

The early Nonconformist building was a house in which to meet for religious worship. The typical chapel interior is still to be found in the back streets of towns and in rural areas: rectangular in plan, including a schoolroom, and with vestries either as part of the original plan or sometimes added later. The pulpit was the focal point of the interior, often elaborately conceived and slightly elevated, with steps on one or both sides and with woodwork of very high quality. The finishings of the Baptist chapel in Tewkesbury, Gloucestershire, are a fine example of Nonconformist craftsmanship and taste. Immediately in front of the pulpit was a rostrum to accommodate the communion table and

chairs and in the main body of the chapel, in front of the rostrum and often separated from it by a brass rail, were provided pews designed for simplicity rather than comfort.

The woodwork of early chapels was usually left in its natural state, but varnished pine was generally used to finish the chapels of the nineteenth century. Around the walls hat pegs were provided for the convenience of the congregation, as can be seen in the Methodist chapel at Elvington in Yorkshire. The modern fashion is to have plain interior walls, but in the days of the Evangelical preachers the walls were embellished with texts and stencilled decorations. Fortunately the use of coloured glass was resisted and it is generally only in Methodist chapels that it can be found today.

Whereas most Nonconformist places of worship achieved a recognisable architectural form, those used by the Quakers never did so. This may be the result of a deliberate policy of eschewing all forms of outward show, due partly to a mistrust of visual arts and partly to persecution in the early days of the movement. The meeting-houses were never dedicated and consequently were used for secular as well as religious purposes. Quakers have always been greatly concerned with education and, after the advent of state education, one or two of the present Quaker schools, such as Ackworth in Yorkshire, trace their foundation to the original meeting-houses.

The typical meeting-house in Bridport in Dorset was originally a barn, adapted to its present use in 1655. The interior has plain walls with wooden benches arranged to form three sides of a square. The fourth side is provided with a table and a bench. In some of the older meeting-houses the fourth side is occupied by a raised bench known as a 'stand' and occupied during worship by the elders. A good example of this arrangement can be found at Wallingford in Oxfordshire. Galleries were sometimes provided, and the space underneath closed off with shutters for the children's meeting or Sunday School; this may be seen at Bridport in Dorset. An occasional feature was the incorporation of a pen, inside the meeting-room, where farmers could leave their dogs during the meeting (Brigflatts, Yorkshire).

The style of building tended to change somewhat in the nineteenth century, when expanding Quaker communities, frequently associated with successful family enterprises, provided funds for new or enlarged meeting-houses. At Street in Somerset a rectangular stone building with a well-proportioned classical portico and cupola was erected, and the meeting-house provided for Ackworth School in 1847 is a building of particular architectural distinction.

Chapter Six

Church
Fittings
and
Furniture

ALTARS

In the mediaeval church the altar was a central object essential to worship. The destruction which took place at the Reformation left few original altar stones surviving, although there have been several instances of altar slabs found being used as paving stones, or in other circumstances of desecration, and subsequently restored to their original use (Peterchurch, Herefordshire).

Originally, altars were made of wood, but in 1076 the Council of Winchester ordered that all altars should be made of stone. A large slab of freestone or marble was levelled and marked with five crosses representing the five sacred wounds of Christ; this was supported on a pedestal (Belper, Derbyshire) or on four or five stone columns (Forthampton, Gloucestershire). At Abbey Dore in Herefordshire the side altar, supposedly of Norman date, stands on three legs, and the altar at Belper in Derbyshire is supported on brackets.

Most altars, when originally consecrated, were provided with a cavity for the reception of sacred relics, usually within the central supporting column or near the front edge, below the central cross. Some of these cavities have survived (Collington, Cornwall; St Robert's Chapel,

Sunningwell, Berkshire
Elizabethan communion table

Knaresborough). Incised altar stones are rare (Camborne, Cornwall).

The Elizabethan injunction of 1559 permitted but did not order the removal of altar stones. Nevertheless in most cases tables or altars of wood were substituted after this date for the stone originals. A number of fine Elizabethan tables with bulbous 'melon' legs have survived (Blyford, Suffolk; Dinton, Bucks). At Townstall in Devon the Elizabethan carved legs take the form of allegorical beasts and at Haddenham in Cambridgeshire the Elizabethan altar table stands on seven legs.

Jacobean tables were generally simpler than their Elizabethan counterparts, although the rails were often decorated with carving and occasionally inscribed with the names of the donors and dates, or an appropriate text (Evesham, Worcestershire; Burton Bassett, Buckinghamshire). At Powick in Worcestershire an example survives of a draw-table which extends from 9 foot 3 inches to 16 foot, and which appears to be a Commonwealth top on an earlier Elizabethan frame. Other examples exist (All Saints, Hereford; Upper Donhead, Wiltshire) and it is likely that these came into being following the issue in 1644 of the *Directory of Worship*, after which the table would have been brought into the body of the church and the communicants would sit round it. After the Restoration, altar tables were replaced in their proper position against the east wall of the chancel and in many cases, the old tables having been either destroyed or removed, new tables were provided, many of them dated (Mainstone, Shropshire; Kirk Ireton, Derbyshire).

Altar Rails

When chancel screens were provided there was little need for altar rails. The necessity for rails, to secure the sanctuary from dogs, became apparent during the reign of Elizabeth, when rood screens or gates were generally removed. Rails at Flintham and Elton in Nottingham-

Langley Chapel, Shropshire
Arrangement of communion table

shire date from this period, although most early examples surviving today date from after the reign of Charles I. The earliest are generally known as 'Laudian' (Winchester Cathedral Lady-chapel), after Archbishop Laud. Generally these early rails were placed across the chancel from north to south (Piddinghoe, Sussex), but examples of three-sided rails have survived (Poynings, Sussex). Rails installed after the restoration of episcopal rule in 1660 generally had spiral balusters (Thurne, Norfolk; Parkham, Devon), those at Lewknor, Oxfordshire, being dated 1699.

Reredos

It was usual to provide behind the altar some special background to enhance its visual impact. This took the form of hangings, paintings or a masonry panel. The earliest were undoubtedly painted murals (St Albans Abbey, Hertfordshire), although the stone carvings at Chichester Cathedral, Sussex, belong to the same date (c. 1200). In the cathedrals and great monastic or collegiate establishments the reredos was usually freestanding and constructed of masonry (Christchurch, Hampshire; Southwark, London). These screens, dating from the second half of the fourteenth century, comprise lofty walls usually of tabernacle-enriched masonry, that at Christchurch incorporating a representation of the tree of Jesse and that at Milton in Hampshire bearing the date of its erection, AD 1492. Whereas most examples extend to the full height of the east wall, low freestanding examples are common (Westminster Abbey; Great Malvern Priory, Worcestershire). At Beverley and Selby in Yorkshire the detached altar screens are of some depth and provide roomy galleries above. At Durham the reredos is constructed in open tabernacle-work some 30 foot high and is returned on each side to form sedilia.

In smaller churches, the east wall of the chancel behind the altar was usually treated as a reredos either by arcading or panelling. In more important examples this work was carried out in masonry (St Peter, Ludlow, Shropshire; Clapton-in-Gordano, Somerset). In many churches there are panels of alabaster, mined at Chellaston in Derbyshire and carved in Nottingham (St Peter Mancroft, Norwich, Norfolk). Wooden reredos are rare but painted panels used for the purpose survive (Gloucester Cathedral; Romsey Abbey, Hampshire). The best example is to be found in Westminster Abbey, probably painted by Master Waller, painter to Edward I. Another fine example is the Norwich reredos, c. 1380, used for many years as a table-top. An example of an oak reredos frame, originally provided to carry hangings or draperies, is to be found in Michaelchurch in Powys.

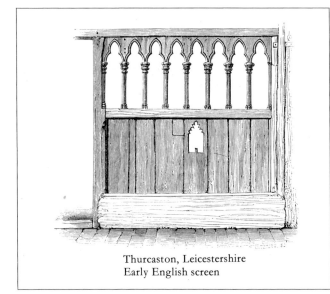

Thurcaston, Leicestershire
Early English screen

SCREENS AND ROOD LOFTS

Chancel and rood screens were more common in England than in any other country in Europe and surviving examples are more plentiful and beautiful than elsewhere. In the Middle Ages most English churches were provided with a screen to separate the clergy from the laity and in many parish churches this was surmounted by a rood. Where the screen was not provided, the rood was carried on a beam. At the Reformation the rood was removed and this often involved the destruction of the rood loft, although in most cases the screens themselves survived – many of them, however, being wantonly destroyed in the course of renovation in the nineteenth century. Screens separating chancels from side aisles, called parcloses, were also often provided, as were screens to chapels and side altars.

In early Saxon churches the small arch between nave and chancel was probably closed off by a curtain or veil, which survived in the mediaeval use in England of the Lenten veil shutting off the view of the altar by a curtain of painted linen. In England the desire to gain a better sight of the altar than that afforded through a small single archway originated the triple chancel arch (Ashley and Otterbourne, Hampshire; Pyecombe, Sussex). Although these mostly date from Norman times, later examples have survived (Westwell, Kent; Wool, Dorset; Welch Newton, Gwent).

Rarely, parish churches followed the example of large minster or conventual buildings with a stone screen and central doorway (Eastwell, Leicestershire). In the small fourteenth-century church at Capel-le-Ferne, near Dover, the wall between the nave and chancel contains an open arcade of two central arches on octagonal shafts, with a further opening over the central arch which originally must have contained the rood. At Great Bardfield in Essex the chancel arch has been filled in with stone tracery dating from the fifteenth century.

During the fifteenth century many stone screens were

removed and replaced with timber screenwork coved at the top to support wide rood lofts. In some cases the original stone screen was adapted to support the new loft (Tintinhull, Somerset). In the larger churches a rood beam separated the sanctuary from the stalls, often with a lighter screen below, in the position of the later altar rails (St David's Cathedral, Dyfed); in small churches, where the chancel arch was low, the rood was fixed to a beam over the crown of the arch, with the eastern wall of the nave as a background (Frindsbury, Kent). When, as in many churches, the original chancel arch was pulled down and a new larger arch inserted, it was common practice to insert a timber tympanum in the upper part of the new arch, often painted as a background to the rood (Ellingham, Hampshire).

In the larger monastic or minster churches stone screens of solid masonry were provided to shut off the choir from the rest of the church. Originally the screen comprised a simple wall pierced by one central or two lateral doorways (Malmsbury Abbey, Wiltshire; Boxgrove Priory, Sussex; Crowland Abbey, Lincolnshire), but later examples comprised a mass of masonry of some thickness supporting a gallery to which access was provided by an internal staircase (Southwell Minster, Nottinghamshire). Many of these screens, to which the name 'pulpitum' is usually applied, are enriched with architectural ornament, niches, tabernacle-work or panelling (York Minster; Ripon Cathedral, Yorkshire). At Compton Bassett in Wiltshire an open arcade is provided in front of the solid screen, providing lateral altar recesses on either side of the door.

Openwork screens are more common than solid and are mostly found in parish churches. They survived the Reformation despite the removal of their rood, and although of great variety of design, all incorporate the general arrangement of solid base, often with painted panels between upright mullions supporting a stage of openwork with traceried heads. Surmounting the whole was usually an enriched beam, or timber vaulting in imitation of stone ribbing, supporting the gallery. Most screens are of the Perpendicular period but earlier examples have survived at Compton in Surrey (Norman), Stanton Harcourt in Oxfordshire (Early English) and Northfleet in Kent (Decorated). Many fine later screens still enrich parish churches throughout the country (Old Radnor, Patristow, Powys; Castle Acre, Norfolk), but probably the best are to be found in Devonshire, where they often extend the full width of nave and aisles (Haberton, Devon).

Screens continued to be constructed after the Reformation and some incorporate Renaissance details of varying quality. One of the best examples can be seen at Cartmel Priory, Cumbria. St John's, Leeds, Yorkshire, incorporates a vigorous example of the work of this period and the screen provided, c. 1632, by John Abel in the reconstruction of Abbey Dore, Herefordshire, is a fine example of West Country carpentry.

PULPITS

Although pulpits were provided in monastic refectories (Beaulieu Abbey, Hampshire) from an early date, they do not appear to have been provided in parish churches until the fourteenth century. Most pulpits which now survive belong to the Perpendicular period and are constructed of wood or stone.

Stone pulpits are usually polygonal and attached to a pier for support; some are bracketed out from a niche in the wall whose thickness contains the staircase of access (Chipping Sodbury, Gloucester; Nailsea, Somerset). The faces are usually panelled, adorned with tracery and sometimes carved. Apart from Mellar in Derbyshire, where the hexagonal pulpit is cut from a solid block of oak, wooden pulpits are much alike and widely distributed. Each comprises an octagonal or hexagonal tub with panelled sides, supported on a shaft, usually with miniature buttresses and sunk panelling. Many are decorated with colour and gilding (Burnham

Salle, Norfolk
Three-decker pulpit

Norton, Norfolk; Cheddar, Somerset). The fifteenth-century sexagonal pulpit at Fotheringhay in Northamptonshire is provided with a hexagonal fan-vaulted canopy, with the back panelled and incorporating the arms and supporters of Edward IV.

Few Elizabethan pulpits exist and most are undated (Welcombe, Devon). Dated survivals include those at Bungay in Suffolk (1558) and Lenhan in Kent (1574). With the accession of James I came a great surge in pulpit-building and a number of well-carved and handsome pulpits were introduced into parish churches. Fine dated examples survive at Cley in Norfolk (1611), Dent in Yorkshire (1614) and East Dean in Sussex (1621). Sounding-boards became popular, supported on slender carved shafts. The fine pulpit at Trottiscliffe in Kent, originally made for Westminster Abbey, has a shaft carved in the form of a palm tree. Fine dated Carolean pulpits of simple design can be found at Babcary in Somerset (1632), Sedgebrook in Lincolnshire (1634) and Sevenoaks in Kent (1635). Many pulpits bear inscriptions as well as dates, often including the name of the donor and his armorial bearings (Broadwas, Worcestershire; Hope, Derbyshire).

A number of Queen Anne and Georgian pulpits are to be found scattered about the country, mostly in contemporary churches rather than in earlier foundations. Two good examples may be seen at Great Torrington in Devon and Wilverton in Hampshire. Tall, three-decker pulpits were often installed in the galleried churches of the eighteenth century, many of them incorporating the sounding-board originally introduced by Wren in his city churches (St Mary Abchurch, London).

CHURCH SEATING

Thrones

In secular cathedrals a special wooden seat or throne was provided for the bishop on the south side of the choir, east of the stalls. The earliest is probably that at Hereford, and its simplicity is a marked contrast to the splendour of the fourteenth-century throne at Exeter, which rises to a height of 57 feet. At Durham, Bishop Hatfield (1345–81) presented a massive stone structure completely filling the arch of one bay of the choir, with his tomb below and a throne above surmounted by screen and tabernacle-work. At Canterbury is St Augustine's Chair, formed from three pieces of Purbeck marble, and also a wooden chair formerly in the village church of Stanton Bishop, near Bromyard in Herefordshire, where it was known as the Chair of Augustine. At Jarrow-on-Tyne is a chair known as the Chair of the Venerable Bede. All these are of great antiquity, although their exact associations cannot be guaranteed.

Stone seats of undoubted pre-Conquest date survive at Hexham, Northumberland, Beverley Minster, Yorkshire, Barnack, Northamptonshire, and Corhampton, Hampshire. Two further seats of stone of the thirteenth century have survived at Halsham and Sprotborough, both in Yorkshire. Wooden seats of great antiquity exist at Hereford Cathedral, Connington in Cambridgeshire, Lincoln Cathedral and Little Dunmow in Essex. At Bishop Cannings, Wiltshire, is a seat or stall which is an example of a 'carrel', a stall which was provided in the cloisters of monastic institutions to give some convenience and shelter for monks when at study. Two surviving examples of fine coronation chairs are those at Westminster Abbey, incorporating the Stone of Scone, and at York Minster.

After the Reformation it became customary to place one or more chairs, usually of domestic design, within the altar rails. A great number of good Elizabethan and Jacobean chairs, and many of a later date, have survived (Wilmington, Sussex).

Stalls

Sets of stalls were usually provided in churches of monastic or collegiate foundations, or in churches closely connected with them. They do, however, occur in purely parish churches, especially in the east of England (Boston, Lincolnshire). Stalls for the clergy were arranged on either side of the choir in one or sometimes two rows, often with returned stalls at the west end. Each stall was separated from its neighbour by a curved back with elbows and was often provided with a hinged seat whose under-surface incorporated a bracket or misericord to give some support during long periods of standing. In all the large churches except Canterbury the stalls of the back row were covered by canopies, often with a towering spire of openwork (Lincoln Cathedral; Beverley Minster, Yorkshire; Nantwich, Cheshire). In smaller foundations a single continuous canopy was provided (Chichester, Hereford and Bristol Cathedrals; Sherborne, Dorset; Abergavenny, Gwent). Stalls were sometimes set in pairs under a single canopy (Winchester Cathedral) and sometimes in sets of three (St Martin's, Leicester). In the latter case they were probably intended for sedilia.

Only in a few cases were stalls constructed of stone (St Stephen, Norwich and Walpole St Peter, Norfolk), fitted with wooden misericords; most were constructed of wood. The earliest complete set is at Winchester Cathedral (1296) and to the fourteenth century belong the stalls at Boston in Lincolnshire and Ely in Cambridgeshire. Examples at Hereford, Gloucester and Chester Cathedrals date from the fifteenth century. The stalls at Manchester, Bristol, St George's Chapel, Windsor, and Henry VII Chapel, Westminster, were not completed until after 1500. At King's College, Cambridge, are fine

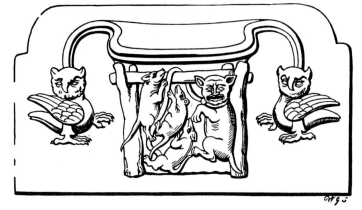

Great Malvern Priory, Worcestershire
Misericord carving: rats hanging cat

stalls belonging to the Renaissance style. Fine ranges of stalls have survived in the parish churches of Minster-in-Thanet, Kent, Ledbury in Herefordshire and Aylesbury in Buckinghamshire.

The misericord carvings show a fine sense of native humour in their subjects. Retributive justice shows a fox being hanged by geese (Beverley Minster) and rats hanging a cat (Great Malvern Priory). Sometimes a fox runs off with a goose (Carlisle Cathedral), pigs play bagpipes (Ripon Cathedral) and fabulous animals, griffins, basilisks and dragons abound. Domestic and agricultural incidents are represented (ploughing at Lincoln Cathedral) and at Boston the schoolmaster birches a boy, to the delight of his fellows.

Benches and pews

As congregations generally stood when they were not kneeling, benches of stone were provided only around the walls, for the elderly and infirm. These benches are common in Cornwall (St Piran) and can also be found scattered generally throughout England (Patrington, Yorkshire; Acton, Cheshire; Hunstanton, Norfolk). Stone seats were usually provided in the porch (Crow-combe, Somerset) and occasionally along the external walls of the church (Craswell, Herefordshire).

The first seating for the general congregation seems to have been provided in chantry parclose or guild chapels, and from there the seating spread generally through the body of the church. The earliest examples were simple benches with terminals, often with carving facing towards the aisle. In western counties the benches usually have square terminals or ends (Broomfield, Somerset), but in East Anglia they end in poppy-heads (South Walsham and St Mary, Norfolk) and in some cases are further enriched by figures in niches. A fine series of stall ends survives at Jarrow-on-Tyne in Durham.

The word 'pew' originally meant an elevated place or seat and came to be applied to seats or enclosures in church for persons of importance. After the Reformation the custom of reserving pews for specific worshippers became common, and they were given lockable doors and curtains in addition to seats and cushions. Many of these pews were the successors of the old chantry parclose which, when its original purpose was abolished, was taken over by the lord of the manor for his own use. A good example is to be seen at Wensley, Yorkshire, where

Stokesay, Shropshire
Canopied pew

the chantry chapel was converted and altered into a pew for the Scrope family in the reign of James I. At Bridgwater, Somerset, is the Corporation pew with screenwork converted from the old rood screen, and at Ightham in Kent are rows of seats enclosed within the original parclose screens. To make the pew more comfortable, the fashion of the seventeenth century was to roof it with a canopy or tester (Stokesay, Shropshire; Madeley, Herefordshire).

GALLERIES

Galleries of pre-Reformation date are not unknown (Cawston and Aylsham, Norfolk) and it is likely that they were used to accommodate singers. These galleries were normally provided beneath the tower, but examples of porch galleries have survived (Clapton, Somerset; Caldecott, Gwent) where the choristers stood who sang the 'Gloria' on Palm Sunday. In the seventeenth century it was common practice to provide galleries to accommodate vocal and instrumental musicians; these usually occupied the west end of the nave, and in time some were extended to the north and south sides of the nave, restricting the light and causing much alteration and damage to the fabric. Most of these have been removed, but many earlier examples have fortunately survived (Lyme Regis, Dorset; Odiham, Hampshire). In some cases galleries have been appropriated for the use of the

Craswell, Herefordshire
The gallery

Burghill, Herefordshire
The font

local landowner (Craswell, Herefordshire) and include not only comfortable seating but also fireplaces to keep the occupants warm.

CHURCH CHESTS

Chests were in common use throughout the Middle Ages for the safekeeping of vestments and valuables. The oldest chests were formed from the solid timber (Fingrinhoe, Essex), and many early examples were made of heavy planks of oak, strongly clamped and bound with iron. Most of the latter date from the fourteenth century and many have carved tops (Cheshunt, Hertfordshire). Often chests were decorated with ornamental iron scroll-work (Icklington, Suffolk) and at Rugby, Warwickshire, the chest is provided with four wheels and rings for poles and carrying-chains. Panelled and carved chests, many of the Elizabethan period or later, are often found to be dated (Chelmorton, Derbyshire, 1630; Wem, Shropshire, 1686).

FONTS

A very large number of Norman fonts, both plain and decorated, are still to be found in English churches. It was not until the fifteenth century that there was a general remaking of fonts, and it appears that it was then the plainer Norman work that was replaced.

In the eleventh and twelfth centuries unmounted fonts (Ibstone, Buckinghamshire) were less common than the mounted types. The former are usually circular, very rarely square or hexagonal. Mounted fonts rest on supports which are constructional and this is characteristic of the Cornish font. The number of supports varies; the font at Bodmin in Cornwall has five supports. Mounted Norman fonts may, in the case of the monopod pattern, be bipartite or tripartite, the former being

without a central stalk and, in the case of the Herefordshire Celtic font, resting on an inverted bowl (Eardisley, Herefordshire). In the Aylesbury type of font, the bowl rests on an inverted capital (Great Kimble, Buckinghamshire). Norman fonts can best be identified by their mouldings and ornament. Examination of the mouldings, where they exist, especially those of the bases and capitals of the shafts and detail of the ornament, provides the best guide. It must be remembered that most fonts were made and placed in position some time after the main details and mouldings were incorporated in the building. Fonts in general can therefore be assigned later dates than similar structural details.

1   The string course is usually a semi-circular roll (Binsted, Sussex). This may be carved with the cable ornament familiar to both the Saxon and Norman mason (Eydon, Northamptonshire). The band of cable is sometimes replaced by interlacings (Chaddesley Corbett, Worcestershire).
2   Arcading was used to enshrine statues or representations of apostles and similar subjects (Darenth, Kent). This pattern of decoration was followed in several of the lead fonts (Brookland, Kent). Where the arcading is composed of intersecting arches and is the sole or prime motif of the design (Hendon, Middlesex), the work is of a later period.
3   The shafts are usually cylindrical and are frequently spiral-grooved (Burnham Norton, Norfolk). This decoration indicates twelfth-century work.
4   The capitals are of Norman patterns, Corinthianesque (Kilpeck, Herefordshire), undivided cushion (Avebury, Wiltshire) and the scalloped capital (Darenth, Kent). Later work incorporates the water-leaf or plantain leaf capital. The water-leaf occurs at Crambe, Yorkshire, and plantain leaves which were in use between 1165 and 1190 are found in Tournai marble fonts (East Meon, Hampshire). The bases of Aylesbury fonts take the form of a scalloped capital.

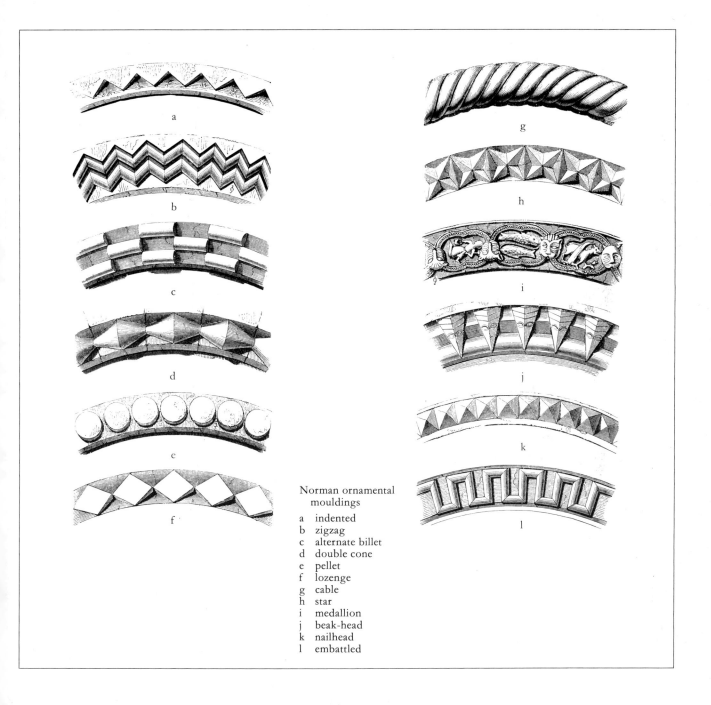

Norman ornamental
  mouldings

a indented
b zigzag
c alternate billet
d double cone
e pellet
f lozenge
g cable
h star
i medallion
j beak-head
k nailhead
l embattled

5 The base mouldings, where these are provided, are important. They commonly consist of two rolls separated by a side hollow. In later examples the deep hollow gradually developed into the undercut 'water-holding' hollow of early Gothic (Crambe, Yorkshire).

6 The spur or griffe was a great favourite and in the Aylesbury fonts assumes a foliated form (Great Kimble, Buckinghamshire).

Norman ornament is both rich and diversified. Interlacings appear in great profusion after 1090, and where they are elaborate they are probably survivals of Saxon or Celtic design traditions. Examples of this elaboration are found in the Hereford Celtic group (Eardisley, Herefordshire) and an allied series in north-west Norfolk (Castle Rising, Norfolk). Interlacing snakes sometimes appear (Bodmin, Cornwall) and pearl ornament is common on bands or scrolls (Lewknor, Oxfordshire). Scrolls, or rinceaux, were in great favour and in some cases they can be attributed to the importation through Normandy of Roman leaf scrolls or acanthus leaves. They may be seen on the faces of scallops of the Aylesbury base (Aylesbury, Buckinghamshire). All the other types of Norman ornament, pellet, herringbone, sawtooth and nailhead, may be found on fonts throughout the country; the exception is chevron, or zigzag, moulding which, however, was used in profusion on the orders of arches to windows, piers and doorways of the twelfth century.

Figure sculpture is very rich and abundant. These sculptured fonts must have been greatly admired by later generations for so many of them to have survived. The choice of subject, as may be expected, is mainly biblical, and the most commonly found is the life of Christ (Castle Frome, Herefordshire). Another favourite was Old Testament stories such as King David and his harp (Darenth, Kent), or the story of Adam and Eve (East Meon, Hampshire). The story of St Nicholas (St Nicholas, Brighton, Sussex) and St Michael were also popular subjects. Masks are very common, being usually placed at the corners of the bowl (Launceston, Cornwall). The lion, as the symbol of St Mark, is also popular (Eardisley, Herefordshire) and some fonts rest on animals (Castle Frome, Herefordshire). The lead font at Brookland in Kent contains not only the signs of the Zodiac but also illustrations of the months, copied, no doubt, from a manuscript calendar at the beginning of a psalter.

As may be expected, a good deal of Romanesque design lingered on into the thirteenth century. This is clear from some Cornish fonts. The characteristic thirteenth-century design may be divided into two classes: those made from the shell marble of Purbeck, Petworth or Bethersden, and similar designs in freestone.

Marble fonts usually have octagonal or square bowls resting on four or five legs. Sometimes the bowl is plain (Aldenham, Hertfordshire), normally it is relieved with shallow arcading which may be pointed (Nassington, Northamptonshire), trefoiled (Buxted, Sussex) or semicircular (Battle, Sussex). Shell fonts were very popular and can be found in great numbers, especially where a navigable river facilitated transport. In the fourteenth century there was a great factory at Purbeck which produced not only marble fonts but also column shafts, bases and annulets. It is surprising to find such plain and simple fonts after the rich examples of the previous century, but the polished face of the marble must have compensated for the lack of surface decoration.

Freestone fonts of this period are not so common, but where they occur their design is more interesting. The bowl is sometimes circular (Barnack, Northamptonshire), sometimes square (St Giles, Oxford). It may be octagonal (Hadleigh, Essex) or hexagonal (Etchingham, Sussex). There is also a curious and beautiful series of cup fonts (Shere, Surrey). The earliest fonts had detached supporting shafts (Barnack) but, reflecting architectural development, later fonts have engaged shafts. The most striking feature of these later fonts is the economy with

Above left: All Saints, East Meon, Hampshire
Above right: St Mary, Eastbourne, Sussex
Left: Weston Turville, Buckinghamshire

which ornament was used. Nailhead or tooth ornament is infrequent (St Giles, Oxford), foliated work is sparingly used (Honiton, Devon) and a few examples have continuous tendrils of foliage of Romanesque pattern (Barnack). The reason must be that the Purbeck masons exercised an influence far beyond the limits of their own narrow sphere. Shell marble was not a suitable material for carving intricate ornament and the risk of damage in transit was very real. It was inevitable that these masons should prefer to produce fonts with the minimum of raised ornament. They considered balanced proportions to be of greater importance and this preference contributes in a major degree to the quality of the freestone fonts which have survived.

By the beginning of the fourteenth century, marble had gone out of fashion, although it was still used for tombs of the altar type. Marble-work produced in the previous century had lost its original brilliant polish and masons went back to using the freestones which had previously fallen out of favour. Design now became standardised and, with very few exceptions, the octagonal font, either on an octagonal pedestal or unmounted, typifies the work of this period. This was an era of lavish decoration and nowhere is this found in greater abundance that on the fonts, always employed with perfect taste and of great beauty.

The treatment of the faces of the bowl was carried out in various ways. In the previous century arcading had been considered sufficient and, while in the poorer villages the faces might be left plain, the favourite device now was to employ the niche. Two preferred types were in vogue, the first employing a decorated straight-sided pediment (Wickham Market, Suffolk) and the second the ogee arch which became popular about 1350 (Hitchin, Hertfordshire).

From the latter part of the fourteenth century and up to the Dissolution of the Monasteries a large number of fonts were remade, some simple and plain (Brancaster,

Norfolk) and others magnificent creations such as the series of fonts on which are depicted the seven sacraments. There is, however, less originality in the design, and plagiarism can be noted. The pedestal and tub fonts of the previous century were reduced to a single standardised pattern. This was the octagonal pedestal font which became generally accepted over the whole country.

The main field for design now lay in the rectangular panels of the bowl. These, separated by a shaft, were filled with figure sculpture (Walsoken, Norfolk) or with a pattern composed of rectangular panelling (Cromer, Norfolk). Equal care was given to the pedestal, with ornamental panelling (Trunch, Norfolk) tiers of square flowers (Cromer) or carved figures (Walsingham, Norfolk). Even the faces of the steps were enriched with quatrefoils in circles or squares, and Catherine wheels.

The instruments of the Passion were frequently represented on the panels of the bowl (St Clement's, Hastings). The Holy Trinity and Christ's baptism (Stalham, Norfolk), and the Crucifixion (Aylsham, Norfolk) were also favourite subjects. Many of these fonts show traces of brilliant colour, but the practice of post-Reformation church-wardens in whitewashing fonts, and the scraping which was part of nineteenth-century restoration, have removed most of the varied colouring and gilding. Traces do remain in certain fonts, mainly in East Anglia (East Dereham, Norfolk).

Two groups of fonts deserve special mention, both mainly indigenous to East Anglia. The first is of general fifteenth-century pattern but providing on the panels of the bowl for an arrangement of carved shields, Tudor roses, the symbols of the Evangelists or demi-angels. Around the pedestals stood lions, angels, kings, queens and saints (Oulton, Suffolk). The second group of fonts depict on their bowls the seven sacraments (East Dereham, Norfolk). The order of the sacraments varies and only in a few examples is the normal order observed. Many of the subjects have been defaced and mutilated.

Cley-next-the Sea, Norfolk

All are octagonal pedestal fonts and at Westhall, Suffolk, the font retains some traces of colour and gilding. At Salle, Norfolk, the font has not only the figure scenes but also the emblems below each sacrament.

It was not until some time after the Dissolution that religious changes affected the font, but the impulse of the previous century soon slackened and few fonts were made in the ensuing years. Some were destroyed during the Commonwealth and many others defaced, some being used as farmyard troughs for animals. After the Restoration some churchmen insisted on reverting to the traditional designs. The Gothic craftsman had, however, passed away and his craftsmanship was lost. There were others who had the taste and good sense to realise that Gothic was no longer a living art; men such as Wren provided fine classical fonts which continued the tradition formulated by the anonymous artists who worked in stone to produce the glorious examples of Gothic baptismal font design which are our heritage today.

CHURCH LIBRARIES

Church libraries were re-established in many parish and cathedral churches soon after the Reformation. In many cases libraries had existed in these long before the Dissolution of the Monasteries, so that the vicar and chaplains might be able to study there as they pleased. For security, most of these books were chained to their shelves. In 1537 the Bible in English was provided in churches for the use of congregations, with a desk and chair. A surviving example is to be seen in the library of Lincoln Cathedral. The largest collection of chained books in existence is to be found in the library of Hereford Cathedral where, of two thousand volumes, 1500 are chained. At Cartmel Priory, Cumbria, survives a library of nearly 300 volumes, established in the first half of the seventeenth century, and at All Saints, Hereford, a library of about 200 chained volumes, one of the largest to be found in a parish church.

PISCINA

A piscina is a water-drain placed near to the altar for the dispersal of water used for the washing of the chalice and priest's hands at Mass. In the thirteenth century the preliminary washing of the priests' hands was general, thus two piscina are sometimes found side by side, but this practice lapsed in the succeeding century. Norman examples are not common (Ryarsh, Kent; Scarcliffe, Derbyshire): generally a square stone or a shaft with an ornamented capital projects from the wall (Towersey, Oxfordshire). Many thirteenth-century single piscinas are to be found, often attractively ornamented and of graceful proportions (Bramley and Elvetham, Hampshire). In some churches an angle piscina niche was formed in the eastern jamb of the south chancel window, often with a trefoil head (Blyford, Suffolk). A later fifteenth-century example may be found at Cheltenham, Gloucestershire. Sometimes a stone shelf to support the cruets, or ciborium, anticipating the later credence table, was provided (Swineshead, Huntingdonshire) and a few wooden shelves have survived (Grosmont, Gwent). Double piscinas of the fourteenth century survive at

Castor, Northamptonshire
Piscina

Cowling, Suffolk. Piscinas of the fifteenth century are rare, but a few good examples survive, as at Treborough, Somerset.

SEDILIA

This is the name applied to the three stone seats, or recessed canopy stalls, sometimes to be found in the south wall of the chancel near the altar, and originally for the use of the priest, deacon and sub-deacon at High Mass. The earliest examples are graduated in height (Moneyash, Derbyshire). Sometimes the piscina was integrated in the design (a fine example is to be found at Ilbestone, Derbyshire) and sometimes the dividing walls between the seats are pierced and open (Rotherham, Yorkshire). At Southwold, Suffolk, the seats are not divided but are enclosed by a richly carved canopy running continuously over the whole length of the bench seat. Single sedilia can be found at Ditchling, Sussex, and at Lenham in Kent. Double sedilia occur at Whitwell, Derbyshire, and St Mary's, Bedford. Although

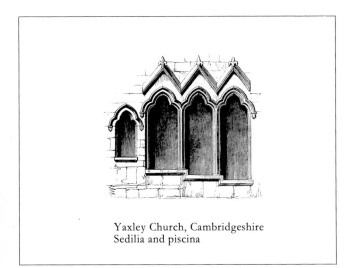

Yaxley Church, Cambridgeshire
Sedilia and piscina

three is the normal number, this has been exceeded: fourfold sedilia at Stratford-on-Avon, Warwickshire, and Ottery St Mary, Devon; five-stalled sedilia at All Saints, Maidstone, Kent, and Southwell Minster, Nottinghamshire.

EASTER SEPULCHRES

These were originally movable chests or receptacles placed on the north side of the chancel on Maundy Thursday and containing a consecrated wafer enclosed in a pyx with a cross. This was watched constantly until, at an early hour on Easter Day, the pyx was removed and placed on the altar. These chests were usually of wood but occasionally a wood framework enriched with hangings was used.

The structural recess known as the Easter sepulchre appears to have come into use in the later thirteenth century and most belong to the Decorated period. They are invariably found on the north side of the chancel, or in the north aisle if the chancel is fully aisled. Usually the recess was at floor level and enclosed by a cusped and crocketed arch. Some are provided with tracery and tabernacle-work and many are of great height (Bampton, Oxfordshire; Northwold, Norfolk). In Lincolnshire are to be found many sculptured sepulchres: Lincoln Cathedral has sculptured soldiers of the thirteenth century and Heckington a sculptured representation of the Resurrection. Another fine example, at Hawton, Nottinghamshire, contains various sculptured groups of sleeping soldiers, the Rising from the Tomb, the Visit of the Marys and the Ascension.

The niche was sometimes designed to be used as an individual memorial as well as for the Easter sepulchre. The memorial to Lord Dacre on the north side of the chancel to Herstmonceux, Sussex, was for this specific purpose. In other cases the sepulchre assumes the form of a chest tomb, often with panelled work and bearing the symbols of the Passion (Porlock, Somerset).

LECTERNS

Churches of the Middle Ages were provided with lecterns from which the Gospel was read. They were usually movable, being constructed of wood or metal, more rarely of stone. Movable lecterns are either a simple desk supported on a pillar or are in the form of an eagle or a pelican supporting the book on outstretched wings. The desk is the earlier form, dating from the thirteenth to the fourteenth centuries, the eagle from the fifteenth to the sixteenth centuries.

The eagle type was revived in the seventeenth century and examples survive in Wells (1660), Lincoln (1667) and York (1666). A metal desk may be found at Yeovil, Somerset, and the best wooden examples include those at Detling, Kent, and Lingfield, Surrey. Early metal eagles can be found at King's College, Cambridge, and Oundle, Northamptonshire.

Stone desks are rare, but examples may be found at Much Wenlock Priory, Shropshire, and at Crowle in Worcestershire, both from the thirteenth century. Stone lecterns comprising a small desk projecting from the north wall of the chancel occur mainly in Derbyshire (Crick; Mickleover; Taddington) and also at Roos, Yorkshire, and Chipping Warden, Northamptonshire.

The choirs of some larger churches were provided with double desks to support large music-books for antiphonal singing. An example survives at Blythburgh, Suffolk, and another at Shipdham, Norfolk.

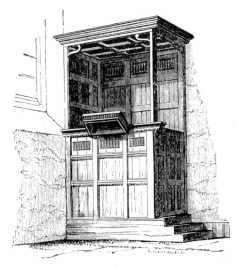

Langley Chapel, Shropshire
Seventeenth-century reading pew

Appendix

Church Buildings Mentioned in the Text

SOUTH WEST ENGLAND
The Greater Churches

Avon	Bath Abbey
Cornwall	Truro Cathedral
Devon	Exeter Cathedral
Dorset	Wimborne Minster
Gloucestershire	Gloucester Cathedral
	Tewkesbury Abbey
Somerset	Wells Cathedral
Wiltshire	Salisbury Cathedral

Abbeys and Conventual Houses

Avon	Bristol Cathedral
Dorset	Sherborne Abbey
Gloucestershire	Cirencester Abbey
	Gloucester Cathedral
	Tewkesbury Abbey
Somerset	Cleeve Abbey, Watchet
	Forde Abbey, Chard
	Glastonbury Abbey
	Mulchelney Abbey, Langport
	Wells Cathedral
Wiltshire	Lacock Abbey, Chippenham
	Malmesbury Abbey
	Salisbury Cathedral

Parish Churches

Cornwall	St Patrick, Bodmin
	Lelant
	Launceston
	St Stephen-by-Saltash
	Veryan
Devon	Higher Bickington
	Ippleden
	Ottery St Mary
Dorset	St Mary, Blandford
	Melbury Bubb
	Sherborne Abbey
Gloucestershire	Chipping Camden
	Cirencester Abbey
	Deerhurst
	Northleach
	Thornbury
Somerset	Compton Bishop
	Doulting
	Huish Episcopi
	Wrington
Wiltshire	Bradford-on-Avon

The Construction of Churches

Avon	Bath Abbey
	Bristol Cathedral
	St Mary Redcliffe, Bristol
Cornwall	Lelant
Devon	Exeter Cathedral
Dorset	Sherborne Abbey
Gloucestershire	Chipping Camden
	Elkstone
	Gloucester Cathedral
	Tewkesbury Abbey
Somerset	Wells Cathedral
	St Cuthbert, Wells
Wiltshire	Malmesbury Abbey
	Salisbury Cathedral

Nonconformist Chapels and Meeting Houses

Dorset	Friends Meeting House, Bridport
Gloucestershire	Baptist Church, Stow-on-the-Wold
	Baptist Church, Tewkesbury
Somerset	Friends Meeting House, Street
Wiltshire	Congregational Chapel, Horningsham
	Hay Lane Chapel, Wootton Bassett

Church Fittings and Furniture

Avon	Bristol Cathedral
Cornwall	Bodmin
	Camborne
	Collington
	Launceston
	St Piran
Devon	Exeter Cathedral
	Great Torrington
	Haberton
	Honiton
	Ottery St Mary
	Parkham
	Townstall
	Welcombe
Dorset	Lyme Regis
	Sherborne Abbey
	Wool
Gloucestershire	Cheltenham
	Chipping Sodbury
	Forthampton
	Gloucester Cathedral

Somerset	Babcary
	Bridgwater
	Broomfield
	Cheddar
	Clapton
	Clapton-in-Gordano
	Crowcomb
	Nailsea
	Porlock
	Tintinhull
	Treborough
	Wells Cathedral
	Yeovil
Wiltshire	Avebury
	Bishop Cannings
	Compton Bassett
	Malmesbury Abbey
	Upper Donhead

LONDON AND SOUTH EAST

The Greater Churches

Buckinghamshire	Wing Parish Church
Hampshire	Beaulieu Abbey
	Christchurch Priory
	Winchester Cathedral
Hertfordshire	St Albans Abbey
Kent	Bayham Abbey, Lamberhurst
	Canterbury Cathedral
	Rochester Cathedral
London	St Paul's Cathedral
	Cathedral of St George, Southwark
	Westminster Abbey
	Westminster Cathedral

Oxfordshire	Oxford Cathedral
Surrey	Guildford Cathedral
Sussex	Chichester Cathedral
	Lewes Priory

Abbeys and Conventual Houses

Hampshire	Beaulieu Abbey
	Christchurch Priory
	Romsey Abbey
	Winchester Cathedral
Hertfordshire	St Albans Abbey
Kent	Bayham Abbey, Lamberhurst
	Canterbury Cathedral
	Minster Abbey, Sheppey
London	Westminster Abbey
	St Margaret's, Westminster
Oxfordshire	Oxford Cathedral
Surrey	Waverley Abbey, Farnham
Sussex	Battle Abbey
	Lewes Priory
	Michelham Priory, Hailsham

Parish Churches

Bedfordshire	Shillington
Buckinghamshire	Bletchley
	Fingest
	Stewkley
	Wing
Hampshire	Hurstbourne
	Milford
	Odiham
	Old Basing

Hertfordshire	Hemel Hempstead
Kent	Brookland
	Hythe
	Mereworth
	New Romney
	Otford
	St Nicholas, Rochester
	St Charles the Martyr, Tunbridge Wells
	Westham
	Wrotham
London	St Anne, Limehouse
	St Anne, Soho
	St Augustine, Kilburn
	St Clement Danes
	St George, Bloomsbury
	St James, Piccadilly
	St John, Smith Square
	St Luke, Chelsea
	St Martin-in-the-Fields
	St Mary Abbott, Kensington
	St Mary-le-Strand
	St Mary Woolnoth
	St Paul, Covent Garden
	St Paul, Deptford
	St Peter, Vere Street
	Queen's Chapel, St James's Palace
	The Temple Church
	Westminster Abbey
Oxfordshire	Burford
	Chipping Norton
	Witney
	Yelford
Sussex	Alfriston
	Bishopstone
	St Peter, Brighton

Clymping
St Saviour, Eastbourne
East Grinstead
Glynde
Hankham
St Clement, Hastings
Littlington
Old Shoreham
Piddinghoe
Sompting
Southcase
Wilmington
Worth

The Construction of Churches

Berkshire	St George's Chapel, Windsor
Hampshire	Christchurch Priory
	Romsey Abbey
	Winchester Cathedral
Kent	Canterbury Cathedral
	St Charles the Martyr,
	Tunbridge Wells
London	Southwark Cathedral
	St John's Chapel,
	Tower of London
	Westminster Abbey
	Westminster Abbey,
	Henry VII Chapel
Oxfordshire	Adderbury
	Oxford Cathedral
Sussex	Boxgrove Priory, Chichester
	Chichester Cathedral
	New Shoreham
	Rye
	South Harting

West Dean
Wilmington

Nonconformist Chapels and Meeting Houses

Hertfordshire	New Mill Baptist, Tring
Oxfordshire	Friends Meeting House,
	Wallingford
Sussex	Unitarian Church, Brighton

Church Fittings and Furniture

Bedfordshire	St Mary, Bedford
	Swineshead
Berkshire	St George's Chapel, Windsor
Buckinghamshire	Aylesbury
	Burton Bassett
	Dinton
	Great Kimble
	Ibstone
Hampshire	Ashley
	Beaulieu Abbey
	Bramley
	Christchurch Priory
	Corhampton
	East Meon
	Ellingham
	Elvetham
	Milton
	Odiham
	Otterbourne
	Romsey Abbey
	Winchester Cathedral
	Winchester Cathedral,
	Lady-chapel
	Wolverton

Hertfordshire	Aldenham		Buxted
	Cheshunt		Chichester Cathedral
	Hitchin		Ditchling
	St Albans Abbey		East Dean
			Etchingham
Kent	Brookland		St Clement, Hastings
	Canterbury Cathedral		Herstmonceux
	Capel-le-Ferne		Piddinghoe
	Darenth		Poynings
	Detling		Pycombe
	Frindsbury		Wilmington
	Ightham		
	Lenham		
	All Saints, Maidstone		
	Minster-in-Sheppey		
	Minster-in-Thanet		
	Northfleet		
	Ryarsh		
	Sevenoaks		
	Trottiscliffe		
	Westwell		

WEST MIDLANDS AND WALES

The Greater Churches

Gwent	Llanthony Priory
Herefordshire	Abbey Dore
	Hereford Cathedral
Powys	Brecon Cathedral
Warwickshire	Coventry Cathedral
Worcestershire	Great Malvern Priory
	Pershore Abbey
	Worcester Cathedral

London — St Mary Abchurch; Southwark Cathedral; Westminster Abbey

Middlesex — Hendon

Oxfordshire — Bampton; Lewknor; St Giles, Oxford; Stanton Harcourt; Towersey

Surrey — Compton; Lingfield; Shere

Sussex — Battle; Binstead; Boxgrove Priory; St Nicholas, Brighton

Abbeys and Conventual Houses

Glamorganshire	Ewenny Priory, Bridgend
	Margam Abbey
Gwent	Llanthony Priory
	Tintern Abbey
Herefordshire	Abbey Dore
	Hereford Cathedral
Shropshire	Buildwas Abbey, Ironbridge
	Much Wenlock Priory

Parish Churches

Gwent	Skenfrith
Herefordshire	All Saints, Hereford
	Kilpeck
	Ledbury
	Madley
	Pembridge
	Ross-on-Wye
	Weobley
Powys	Old Radnor
Shropshire	Clun
Staffordshire	Stafford
Warwickshire	St Nicholas, Warwick
Worcestershire	Great Witney
	Pirton
	Tetbury

The Construction of Churches

Dyfed	St David's Cathedral
Gwent	Tintern Abbey
Herefordshire	Abbey Dore
	Hereford Cathedral
	Leominster Priory
	Rowlstone
Powys	Brecon Cathedral
Shropshire	Bridgnorth
Staffordshire	Lichfield Cathedral
Worcestershire	Evesham
	Great Malvern Priory
	Pershore Abbey
	Worcester Cathedral

Nonconformist Chapels and Meeting Houses

Powys	Maesroenan Congregational Chapel

Church Fittings and Furniture

Dyfed	St David's Cathedral
Gwent	Abergavenny
	Caldecott
	Grosmont
	Welch Newton
Herefordshire	Abbey Dore
	Castle Frome
	Craswell
	Eardisley
	All Saints, Hereford
	Hereford Cathedral
	Kilpeck
	Ledbury
	Madeley
	Peterchurch
	Stanton Bishop
Powys	Michaelchurch
	Old Radnor
	Patristow
Shropshire	St Peter, Ludlow
	Mainstone
	Much Wenlock Priory
	Stokesay
	Wem
Warwickshire	Rugby
	Stratford-on-Avon
Worcestershire	Broadwas
	Chaddesley Corbett
	Crowle
	Evesham
	Great Malvern Priory
	Powick

EAST MIDLANDS

The Greater Churches

Derbyshire	Repton Parish Church
Lincolnshire	Lincoln Cathedral
Nottinghamshire	Newark Parish Church
	Southwell Minster

Abbeys and Conventual Houses

Lincolnshire	Crowland Abbey
	Sempringham Abbey
	Thornton Abbey

Parish Churches

Derbyshire	Baslow
	Chesterfield
	Chilmarton
	Melbourne
	Repton
	Tideswell
Leicestershire	Leicester Cathedral
Lincolnshire	Barton-on-Humber
	Boston
	Grantham
	Long Sutton
	Threckingham
Northamptonshire	Brixworth
	Islip
	Kettering
	Ketton
	St Sepulchre, Northampton
	Oundle
Nottinghamshire	Hawton
	St Mary, Nottingham

The Construction of Churches

Derbyshire	Chesterfield
Leicestershire	Ketton
Lincolnshire	Lincoln Cathedral
Northamptonshire	Higham Ferrers
Nottinghamshire	Southwell Minster

Nonconformist Chapels and Meeting Houses

Lincolnshire	Wesleyan Chapel, Louth

Church Fittings and Furniture

Derbyshire	Belper
	Chelmorton
	Crick
	Hope
	Ilbestone
	Kirk Ireton
	Mellar
	Mickleover
	Moneyash
	Scarcliffe
	Taddington
	Whitwell
Leicestershire	Eastwell
	St Martins, Leicester
Lincolnshire	Boston
	Crowland Abbey
	Heckington
	Lincoln Cathedral
	Sedgebrook
Northamptonshire	Barnack
	Chipping Warden

	Eydon
	Fotheringhay
	Nassington
	Oundle
Nottinghamshire	Elton
	Flintham
	Hawton
	Southwell Minster

EAST ANGLIA

The Greater Churches

Cambridgeshire	Ely Cathedral
	King's College Chapel, Cambridge
	Peterborough Cathedral
Norfolk	Binham Priory
	St Nicholas, King's Lynn
	Norwich Cathedral
	Walsingham Abbey
Suffolk	Bury St Edmunds Abbey

Abbeys and Conventual Houses

Essex	St Osyth's Priory, Clacton
	Waltham Abbey
Norfolk	Castle Acre Priory
	Norwich Cathedral
	Thetford Priory
Suffolk	Bury St Edmunds Abbey

Parish Churches

Cambridgeshire	Holy Sepulchre, Cambridge

Essex	Dedham
	Ingatestone
	Maplescombe
	St Osyth
	Woodham Walter
Norfolk	Bessingham
	Billockby
	Castle Acre
	Cley
	Hales
	Hardingham
	St Margaret's, King's Lynn
	St Nicholas, King's Lynn
	Little Ellingham
	Salle
	Thornage
	West Walton
Suffolk	Dennington
	Eye
	Lavenham
	Long Melford
	Southwold

The Construction of Churches

Cambridgeshire	Ely Cathedral
	Kings College Chapel, Cambridge
	March
	Peterborough Cathedral
Essex	Bocking
Norfolk	Binham Priory
	Necton
	Norwich Cathedral
	Terrington St Clement
Suffolk	Long Melford
	Lavenham

Nonconformist Chapels and Meeting Houses

Norfolk	Octagon Chapel, Norwich
Suffolk	Friar Street Chapel, Ipswich
	Congregational Chapel, Walpole

Church Fittings and Furniture

Cambridgeshire	King's College Chapel, Cambridge
	Connington
	Ely Cathedral
	Haddenham
Essex	Fingrinhoe
	Great Bardfield
	Hadleigh
	Little Dunmow
Norfolk	Aylsham
	Brancaster
	Burnham Norton
	Castle Acre
	Castle Rising
	Cawston
	Cley
	Cromer
	East Dereham
	Hunstanton
	Northwold
	Norwich Cathedral
	St Peter Mancroft, Norwich
	St Stephen, Norwich
	St Mary
	Salle
	Shipdham
	South Walsham
	Stalham
	Thurne

	Trunch
	Walpole St Peter
	Walsingham
	Walsoken
Suffolk	Blyford
	Blythburgh
	Bungay
	Cowling
	Icklington
	Oulton
	Southwold
	Westhall
	Wickham Market

NORTH WEST ENGLAND

The Greater Churches

Lancashire	Liverpool Anglican Cathedral
	Liverpool Cathedral of Christ the King

Abbeys and Conventual Houses

Cheshire	Chester Cathedral
Cumbria	Carlisle Cathedral

Parish Churches

Cheshire	Nether Peover

The Construction of Churches

Cheshire	Chester Cathedral

Church Fittings and Furniture

Cheshire	Acton
	Chester Cathedral
	Nantwich
Cumbria	Cartmel Priory
	Carlisle Cathedral
Lancashire	Manchester Cathedral

NORTH EAST ENGLAND

The Greater Churches

Durham	Durham Cathedral
Northumberland	Hexham Priory
	Lindisfarne Priory
Yorkshire	Beverley Minster
	Byland Abbey, Thirsk
	Fountains Abbey, Ripon
	Halifax Parish Church
	Jervaulx Abbey, Masham
	Ripon Cathedral
	Wakefield Cathedral
	York Minster

Abbeys and Conventual Houses

Northumberland	Hexham Priory
Yorkshire	Byland Abbey, Thirsk
	Fountains Abbey, Ripon
	Rievaulx Abbey, Helmsley
	Selby Abbey
	Walton Abbey

Parish Churches

Durham	Darlington
	Escomb
	Monkswearmouth
Yorkshire	Adel
	Cottingham
	Coxwold
	Filey
	Halifax
	Kirk Sandal
	St John's, Leeds
	Rotherham
	Thirsk
	Tickhill

The Construction of Churches

Durham	Durham Cathedral
Northumberland	Hexham Abbey
Yorkshire	Beverley Minster
	Kirkstall Abbey, Leeds
	Ripon Cathedral
	York Minster

Nonconformist Chapels and Meeting Houses

Yorkshire	Friends Meeting House, Ackworth School
	Methodist Chapel, Elvington
	Friends Meeting House, Brigflatts

Church Fittings and Furniture

Durham	Durham Cathedral
	Jarrow-on-Tyne

Northumberland	Hexham
Yorkshire	Beverley Minster
	Crambe
	Dent
	Halsham
	St Robert's Chapel, Knaresborough
	St John, Leeds
	Patrington
	Ripon
	Roos
	Rotherham
	Selby
	Sprotborough
	Wensley
	York Minster

SCOTLAND

The Greater Churches

Lanarkshire	Glasgow Cathedral

Index

Index